T0305834

New Paradigm
for Interpreting the
Chinese Economy

Theories, Challenges and Opportunities

Series on Chinese Economics Research

(ISSN: 2251-1644)

Series Editors: Yang Mu *(Lee Kuan Yew School of Public Policies, NUS)*
Fan Gang *(Peking University, China)*

Series on Chinese Economics Research – Vol. 7

New Paradigm for Interpreting the Chinese Economy

Theories, Challenges and Opportunities

Justin Lin Yifu

The World Bank & Peking University, China

社会科学文献出版社
SOCIAL SCIENCES ACADEMIC PRESS (CHINA)

World Scientific

Published by

World Scientific Publishing Co. Pte. Ltd.

5 Toh Tuck Link, Singapore 596224

USA office: 27 Warren Street, Suite 401-402, Hackensack, NJ 07601

UK office: 57 Shelton Street, Covent Garden, London WC2H 9HE

Library of Congress Cataloging-in-Publication Data

Lin, Justin Yifu, 1952–

   New paradigm for interpreting the Chinese economy : theories, challenges and opportunities /
Justin Lin Yifu.

       pages cm. -- (Series on Chinese economics research ; v. 7)

   Includes bibliographical references and index.

   ISBN 978-9814522311 (alk. paper)

   1. China--Economic conditions--21st century. 2. China--Social conditions--21st century.

3. China--Economic policy--21st century. 4. Financial institutions--China--Management. I. Title.

   HC427.95.L5746 2014

   330.951--dc23

                                                              2013048377

British Library Cataloguing-in-Publication Data

A catalogue record for this book is available from the British Library.

解读中国经济没有现成模式

Originally published in Chinese by Social Sciences Academic Press (China).

Copyright © 2011 Social Sciences Academic Press (China).

In-house Editor: DONG Lixi

Typeset by Stallion Press

Email: enquiries@stallionpress.com

Printed in Singapore

Preface

Contemporary Chinese economists currently exist in a fortuitous time. Previously, because of the political chaos before the foundation of New China, economists could not give full play to their talent or discuss economic development. Fortunately, contemporary Chinese intellectuals, economists in particular, are free to research on various situations, analyze numerous problems, propose policies to strengthen the country that would enhance the livelihood of its people, and participate in many spirited debates. Since the reform and opening up in 1978, Chinese economy has grown rapidly, despite having to rebuild the damaged ruins of the past 150 years. In addition, never-before-seen diversified social and economic phenomena have emerged.

China's gross domestic product (GDP) has grown 12.2 times from 1978 to 2005, with an average annual rate of 9.4%, making it the country of fastest economic growth in this current period. Meanwhile, China also witnessed an annual growth rate of 17% and the gross amount of international trade grew 68 times. China has become the second largest trading country and has seen an average annual rate of 25% after its entry into the World Trade Organization (WTO). China has become the focus of the world in every aspect of its economy, owing to its astonishing achievements and its significant role in the world economy. In world's economic development history, many unique situations have appeared in China's transformation, which cannot be explained with current economic theories. For example, China's rapid growth was doubted by many foreign economists because of the currency deflation and decrease in energy consumption between 1998 and 2002. They raised questions and demonstrated their conclusions based on the then prevalent international economic theories. However, through ordinary relations in the figures of contradiction and practical basis, a conclusion was formed—the impossible has taken place in China.[1]

Instead of blindly following current foreign theories, the only way to understand contemporary Chinese economy is by seeking the truth out of facts and making a concrete analysis of tangible problems. This is my knowledge gained from recent studies on Chinese economy and the reason for naming this book, *New Paradigm for Interpreting the Chinese Economy: Theories, Challenges, and Opportunities*. Therefore, since no paradigm currently exists that could unravel China's success, new theories would be built. Chinese economists are the most appropriate candidates to build new theories since they have a profound understanding of Chinese society and economy and have an amazing grasp of China's systems and phenomena characteristics. This is a very rare chance, and serious obligation, for Chinese economists to bring forth new ideas in economic theories and contribute to the development of economics.

Indeed, Chinese economists need to overcome many challenges in order to turn this opportunity into reality. Many colleagues in economics are putting unremitting efforts into the process, including dedicated individual studies, as well as group collaborations. In addition, they should also constantly exchange and discuss new ideas, theories, and methods appropriately suited for Chinese economy. This opens a field of various new problems and phenomena, only by which mature theories and systems can be established. The Chinese Economists 50 Forum, founded in 1998, has made many accomplishments in this area, including gathering of top-grade experts and scholars in various fields of Chinese economics to discuss serious and controversial problems and organize platforms such as internal discussions, the Chang'an Forum, and annual meetings of the Chinese Economists 50 Forum. Although the Forum is still young, it has realized numerous research achievements and played an important role in the process of economic reform and development in China. As a member of the First Session Scholar Committee of this Forum, I am gratified and proud to be a part of such an important historical time and I am confident about China's future.

---

[1] See details in Chapter 12 and Sec. 8 of Chapter 12 of this book.

In the past two decades, I have had the honor of being a witness, supporter, and researcher of the contemporary economic reform in China. In 1979, at the beginning of the reform and opening up, I had studied the political economics of socialism at Beijing University for three years and become one of the first scholars that accepted systematic training on economics in the U.S. I then returned to China in the mid-1980s to participate in policy research. Since then, I began to pay attention to various problems in the process of economic development in China's reform and opening up and advocated to analyze these problems using strict economic methods. I have gradually expanded my research scope from rural economics to development strategies, macroeconomy, reform of state-owned enterprises, financial reform, issues concerning agriculture, rural areas and peasants, foreign trade, and the research and teaching of economics. I summarized my research results in many articles, which were partly published in foreign academic periodicals, some domestic economics magazines, research presentations, some seminar speeches, and partly collected in books. In this book, I aim to summarize my research in the various fields of Chinese economy. In order to make this book as complete and thorough as possible, I have collected some representative short articles, research presentations, and speech drafts from several areas in recent years. Although few profound and detailed theoretical analyses can be found in these chapters, they present some individual ideas on the problems of the Chinese economy, solutions to these problems, challenges, and opportunities. Therefore, some cursory analyses may have been made. Here, I have attempted to present an overall view of the challenges and opportunities in the economic reform and development of China and am open to your own interpretation of Chinese economic phenomena.

Contents

Chapter 1

Prospect for the Chinese Economy in the 21st Century — Speech for the 2001 BiMBA Top Management Class of Beijing University

1. Introduction

Three key characteristics encompass a serious entrepreneur: they are meticulous about securing the right place, they seek the support of the people, and they possess the ability to launch their businesses at the right time. The "right place" refers to both the right position and industry; the "support of the people" refers to leading a group to collectively strive toward a common goal; but the "right time" is very difficult to anticipate, so the most important aspect for entrepreneurs is the trend and environment of macro economy.[1] Successful entrepreneurs possess many qualities,

---

[1] Take the most successful entrepreneur in Hong Kong, Li Jiacheng (also called "superman"), as an example. How did he become one of the world's richest men within only two or three decades? A very important factor is the rapid economic growth of Hong Kong. Economics will never develop in a straight direction, but often in a fluctuant way. The key to Li Jiacheng's success is his correct judgment about Hong Kong's long-term economic development. He entered the economic circle when others who lacked confidence chose to leave. During the "Cultural Revolution" in the 1960s, when the Red Guard showed up in Hong Kong and it became easy for the Chinese government to reclaim Hong Kong, many people lost confidence and thus sold real estates in large scale. However, Li Jiacheng was very confident. He mortgaged his plastics factory for bank loans and bought his first real estate. Then he mortgaged it and bought his second real estate. After the "Cultural Revolution" ended, when Hong Kong economy was stabilized and other people came back, he had become a big landlord. After 1984, many people lost confidence in Hong Kong economy, and the stock and real estate market had collapsed. Li Jiacheng was also very confident in Hong Kong's long-term economic development. He bought houses when others sold. Within several years, the house prices were revived and even higher than before.

including proper selection of industry, internal management, and accurate judgment about long-term economic development. Many opportunities lie in the long-term and rapid economic development, along with fluctuations in the process. For entrepreneurs with a correct judgment of long-term economic development, economic fluctuation is the best chance to thrive.

How will Chinese economy develop in the future? There are differing views on this subject. Optimistically, Chinese economy will develop at a rapid rate in future decades. Pessimistically, Chinese economy may collapse any time. The author here reaches an optimistic conclusion on the long-term economic development in China based on his analysis.[2]

2. Review of Achievements in the Chinese Economy After Reform and Opening up

In the study of history, it is necessary to recognize that the past is the basis for the present; one must first understand the current economic status before predicting the future. Here, the author briefly overviews the economic achievements of China after reform and opening up in 1979.

Firstly, in the 22 years between 1979 and 2001, the biggest achievement was in the annual gross domestic product (GDP) growth rate of 9.6% that made China the fastest growing economy during this period.[3] The national economic growth increased approximately 6.8 times — a great economic history phenomenon for a country with such a large population.

Secondly, China has seen an annual growth rate of 14.6% in its total export–import volume in the past 22 years. The export volume of China increased from US$10 billion in 1979 to the present US$230 billion, a

---

[2]The author cannot guarantee the future of Chinese economy, but can only state the understanding and comprehension of the future based on the analysis as an economist.

[3]At the beginning of reform and opening up in 1979, Deng Xiaoping put forward the goal that Chinese economy would grow by four times in two decades. I was a student of Beijing University at that time. I only considered him to be a politician, who proposed a high, or even impossible, aspiration to unite the Chinese to strive for the goal. In 1979, a billion Chinese were living in rural areas. The annual growth rate had to reach 7% to realize the goal. No country as big as China had seen a constant growth rate of 7% over 20 years, so everyone thought that it was impossible. Now, 21 years have passed and the Chinese economy had grown by 6.8 times, much higher than the goal of "four times" put forward by Deng Xiaoping.

growth of 22 times. China's foreign trade dependence was only 9.7% in 1979,[4] compared to 44% of the gross national product (GNP) in 2000, including 23% of export and 21% of import. This figure, which is higher than that of all big countries of the world,[5] is a great achievement for China.

The rapid growth rate in foreign trade and national economy has played an important role in improving the living standards of people, meanwhile contributing greatly to the development of the world.[6]

3. Factors Contributing to China's Rapid Economic Growth

China's economic growth can be analyzed potentially in three aspects: capital accumulation, change in the industrial structure, and technological change. Firstly, input factors mainly include three types: land (including natural resources), labor, and capital. The land figure is fixed and would never increase.[7] Labor is restrained by the growth rate of the population. The

---

[4]The foreign trade dependence is relevantly smaller for big countries. For example, the foreign trade dependence for the U.S., the most important country in world trade, is only around 15%, and the figure for the big trading nation of Japan only amounts to 16%. Therefore, 9.7% was ordinary for China at that time.

[5]I returned to China and worked in the China Rural Development Research Center in 1987. I was quite impressed by the theory of "international circulation by great import and export" in the mid-1980s. The first discussion I attended in the State Department was the maximum levels to which the foreign trade dependence can reach for such a large country as China. I said that China might reach a foreign trade dependence of 25% through efforts with Indonesia, a country with a population over 100 million, as an example, which reached 22% based on its higher development level than China. Everyone felt surprised by my prediction, especially in comparison to America of 12–13% and Japan of 15% at that time. The current figure is 44%.

[6]The most evident case was the worldwide heated discussion on whether RMB would be devalued after the outbreak of the financial crises in Southeast Asia in 1997. As estimated by many people, RMB would be devaluated, which would lead to the competitive depreciation of Eastern Asian countries and more unstable economy. However, RMB did not depreciate and thus enabled the East Asian economy to be stabilized and revived rapidly. It was mainly because of China's considerable foreign exchange reserve and rapid growth of domestic economy. These are the achievements made in the 21-year reform.

[7]Unlike the 18th and 19th centuries when land could be found by exploring overseas colonies, many places are currently engaged in splitting and gaining independence, so the amount of land may be decreased. At best, the land resources are considered to be given.

growth rate of labor in each country may reach 2% at the maximum, while few countries may even reach 3%. Even the natural population increase rate of African countries, which have a rapid population growth, only amounts to less than 3%. It is clear that the population growth contributes insignificantly to the economic growth, with little difference among various countries. The great difference lies in the capital. In some countries and regions, capital can be quickly accumulated. For example, the annual accumulation rate of China in the previous 22 years has reached approximately 40% of GDP, while in East Asia, an area of rapid economic development, the rate is maintained between 30% and 40%. However, in some countries and regions, capitals are not accumulated at all or they can even show a negative growth. Some African countries have no savings and their capital is devaluated owing to the depreciation of their capital stock. The accumulation rate differs greatly between various countries and regions. Therefore, accumulation is the most important factor for judging a country's or region's potential for economic growth. In places of more rapid capital accumulation, there would be more rapid economic development.

Secondly, the potential also depends on the allocation of production factors. The same production factors that are allocated to industrial departments with higher added value would result in higher outputs. The potential of a country's economic growth should be judged based on the possibility of transferring current production factors in industrial departments of lower added value to industrial sectors of higher added value, i.e., the possibility of change in the industrial structure is the main factor for analyzing a country's economic growth rate.

Finally, the potential also depends on technology upgrading. A better technology structure, which has been provided with ample production factors and productive structure, would lead to higher outputs. Technologies that keep changing constantly would increase the outputs and promote economic development.

The most important among these three aspects is the technological change. The former two aspects, i.e., capital accumulation and change in the industrial structure establish the speed of technological change to a considerable degree. Without technological change, the accumulated capital can only incur the decline of a capital's marginal return, so none are willing to accumulate capital owing to a lower capital return. T. W. Schultz stated in his book, *Transforming Traditional Agriculture*, that peasants in traditional areas do not accumulate capital owing to stagnant technologies and low returns of accumulated capital. To transform the traditional agriculture, new technologies should be introduced for a higher return of capital. If the return rate is higher, then the peasants are more willing to accumulate capital. Therefore, in a country or region, the most important factor that determines the speed of the capital accumulation is the speed of technological change. The speed of capital accumulation is undoubtedly rapid based on the constantly changing technologies. Therefore, capital accumulation also reflects the speed of technological change.

The industrial structure is also related to technologies. New industrial sectors of higher added value cannot be initiated without new technologies. The active information industry with high added value is the result of new technologies. A country's or region's industrial structure is largely dependent on technological changes. Rapid technological changes would contribute to the establishment of industries and industrial sectors of high added value with greater possibilities of changes in the industrial structure. Therefore, it is the potential of technological change that becomes the most important factor in analyzing the potential of a country's or region's economic growth.

There are two ways a technological change can occur in countries through different development stages. In most advanced countries, such as the U.S., Japan, and Europe, technological change or technological innovation amounts to technological invention. Since they have already utilized the best and latest technologies, technological innovation is realized by technological invention based on the high quality of their research and development (R&D).

There exists a technology gap between the developing countries, including China, and the developed countries. Developing countries have lower incomes and more backward technologies. They have two methods to achieve technological innovation: R&D, same with developed countries, and the introduction of new technologies from developed countries. Economically, innovation refers to the application of a new technology or the understanding of a specific production, but does not necessarily refer to the latest technologies. When newer ideas replace presently used technologies, then they can be regarded as innovations. Many developing countries are still using technologies that were invented two or three decades ago, so they have plenty of room for technological change.[8]

Which route is better for technological innovation for the developing countries? Technological invention needs great investment and carries a big risk. At most, 5 out of 100 R&D projects can apply for patents. In addition, some technologies with patents do not succeed in the commercial world, because either the products based on the technology are not accepted, they cost too much, or others of a similar patent produce products with lower cost. Therefore, it is expensive and risky to conduct R&D in latest technologies. Of course, the return rate of the project would be very high if the technology is mature, the patent is successfully applied, and the products are accepted by the market. It is easy to create the illusion that R&D has a very high return rate if one considers only a single successful R&D project and ignores the other 99 failed projects. When the cost of the 99 unsuccessful projects is taken into consideration, the investment return rate of R&D of the latest technologies is low.[9] On the one hand, developing countries do not have enough funds to perform many R&D projects. On the other hand, they have a more economic method to realize technological innovation, which is to introduce technologies.

The most expensive aspect in introducing technologies is the cost of patents. How is new technology related to the cost of the patent? In other words, the more current the technology, the higher would be the cost of the patent. Generally, the technology protection term lasts for 20, 15, or 12 years. Since the technological gap between China and developed

---

[8]Several years ago, spindles in the textile industry were broken in Shanghai, because these spindles had been in use since Zhang Jian founded the textile factory over a century before. It was an innovation to replace the spindles with a history of a 100 years with newer spindles invented three or four decades ago.

[9]The founder of Intel said in his book that he is living in a panic. Why? He has to invest US$2 or US$3 billion to research on chips without any certainty of success. If he fails, his investment becomes boondoggle; and in addition, though he has dominated 70% of PC CPU, if he fails in developing new products, advanced micro devices (AMD) may occupy his entire market. This is the predicament for all companies competing in the latest technologies. The company will definitely stop development without new technologies. However, investment on technologies will not necessarily lead to success. Wang and DEC, which were famous in the computer industry in the 1980s, have already disappeared. Why? It may be only because of the failure or delay of several projects of technological invention. Therefore, R&D of latest technologies is featured with high cost and risk.

countries, in some aspects, has exceeded 20, 30, or even 40 years, the patent fee is not needed to introduce a 20-year technology. The patent fee will be higher for a newer patent, but on average, the fee for introducing new technologies accounts for only one-third of the cost, because a patent can be sold to many people and the new technologies can be easily applied to production after invention;[10] and imitation will be encouraged if the patent is too expensive. Therefore, only one-third of the cost of invention is needed for the introduction of technologies. Considering the cost of the 99% failed inventions, the cost for developing countries to carry out technological innovation by introducing technologies only takes up less than 1% of developed countries.

Seemingly, all of the new technologies are invented by developed countries. Is the technological innovation faster in developed countries, or in developing countries, based on introduction of technologies? In fact, the speed of technological change in developing countries is much faster, because developed countries, which mainly rely on R&D, have a limited number of new technologies each year, only amounting to a little proportion in the current total number of technologies. Before 1979, China mainly carried out technological innovation through its own efforts, but after 1979, China started to introduce technologies for various industries, so the number of technological innovations is much greater than developed countries. The economic phenomena in East Asian countries, including Japan and the "Four Little Dragons" in Asia, mainly resulted from their rapid change in industrial structure based on technological introduction.[11] Before 1979, China was very independent. In the 1950s and 1960s, China adopted the

---

[10]It is the same in every industry. Take Viagra in the biomedicine industry as an example. Its chemical composition stimulates the body. However, hundreds of thousands of chemical experiments are needed to find out the exact chemical composition. After the discovery of the chemical composition, every medium-sized pharmaceutical factory in China could produce the medicine. After invention, everyone can produce their own medicines of a little different composition, but with similar effect. Therefore, it is impossible to sell the patent at a very high price.

[11]How many new technologies have been invented by the Japanese in the process of Japan changing from a developing country to one of the countries of highest income? Only a few. The rapid economic growth in Japan was mainly supported by the introduction of technologies. How about the invention of new technologies by the "Four Little Dragons" in Asia? Seldom. However, they have maintained a rapid growth over a long period.

latest technologies in heavy industry and gave priority to the development of heavy industry, aiming to surpass Britain in 10 years and America in 15 years, but economic development was very slow at that time. After 1979, China has abandoned these endeavors, and instead encouraged to process business with materials, samples, or technical drawings supplied by buyers, engaged in compensation trade, promoted foreign trade; and introduced many labor-intensive products mainly from the declining industries of Japan and the "Four Little Dragons" in Asia, which could not be regarded as latest technologies. However, China has seen a rapid economic development and increase in foreign trade in the last 22 years, which is largely because China chose to introduce technologies to maintain rapid economic growth.

How long can the introduction of technologies sustain economic growth? Limited predictions can be made based on economic theories. It is generally believed that the introduction of technologies plays both a positive and negative role for development, but it is hard to define exactly how long the policy can last. However, according to history, Japan had maintained a rapid economic growth for about 40 years through the introduction of technologies from the end of the World War II (WWII) to the mid and late 1980s, while the "Four Little Dragons" in Asia had maintained a rapid economic growth for four decades, from the late 1950s to the East Asian financial crisis in 1997. With a similar mechanism, it is predicted that China can maintain rapid economic growth for at least 50 years. It is not because the Chinese are cleverer than the Japanese and Koreans, but because the technological gap between Japan at the end of WWII and developed countries was smaller than the gap between China and developed countries in 1979. Similarly, the technological gap between the "Four Little Dragons" in Asia in the late 1950s and developed countries was narrower than the gap between China and developed countries in 1979. How is the technological gap judged? It can be well represented by the average income per capita. Higher income often indicates a higher technological level (excluding several oil-rich countries). Obviously, the technological gap between China in 1979 and developed countries was much greater than the technological gap between developed countries and Japan after WWII or the "Four Little Dragons" in Asia. Compared to their 40-year rapid economic growth, the greater technological gap would enable China to maintain rapid economic growth for about 50 years. Therefore, currently, China still has 30 years of rapid economic growth left. After the end of this period, China would most likely have the largest economy in the world. Owing to the potential development for another 20 or 30 years, some foreign enterprises and companies have started to show great interest in China.

Technological potential only supports the possibility that China will maintain a rapid growth of 8%, or more, in the next 30 years by rapid technological change, capital accumulation, and structural change. However, technological potential exists in all developing countries, including China before reform and opening up. Why, then, has development not been realized in China prior to reform and opening up and other developing countries? It was mainly because of certain obstacles. China is not only a developing country but also a country in transformation. Many problems and structural conflicts are revealed in China's transformation from a planned economy to market economy. If these conflicts escalade, it would be difficult to maintain social stability and rapid economic growth by making use of technological gap.

4. Analysis of Key Problems in Chinese Economy

Firstly, the financial system in China is very delicate. The financial system in China is currently based mainly on four state-owned banks, with their capital consuming about 70% of the whole financial system, but the bad debt accounts for a large proportion.[12] China will soon join the World

---

[12]In the High-Level Meeting of China Development Forum held by Development Research Center of the State Department in March 2001, the Minister of Finance and the president of the Central Bank were invited to make reports. Presidents of several world famous enterprises attended this meeting in which the president of Central Bank, Dai Xianglong, stated that the bad debts in China had accounted for 25%. How high is the figure of 25%? In terms of the factors contributing to the Asian financial crisis, the high proportion of bad bank debts led to a lack of confidence in consumers and foreign exchange flight to other countries. Even in the financial crisis of Thailand, the bad debts accounted for less than 20%. The high proportion of bad debts was also an important factor in the financial crisis of Korea, which was also lower than 20%. Then a scholar asked Dai Xianglong: "Mr. Dai, you attended this meeting last year. You also said that the bad debt in the four state-owned enterprises accounted for 25%. However, the Chinese government has established four state-owned asset management companies in 2000, which removed bad debts of about 1,300 billion yuan. Now, after removing the 1,300 billion yuan bad debt, the proportion of bad debt is still 25% this year. There now exists only two possibilities: the first is that the proportion of bad debts accounted for at least 40% in 2000 instead of 25% as released last year; and the second possibility is that the bad debt of 1,300 billion yuan is immediately formed after the first 1,300 billion yuan has been removed". One way or the other, 25% is a frightening figure.

Trade Organization (WTO) and it is expected that foreign banks would enter China's market. According to the agreement, foreign banks can set up their branches in China, finance RMB businesses and debit and credit of companies in two years, and accept personal savings and loans in five years. Their capital and financial accounts cannot be controlled as before. In this case, the bad debts may possibly lead to the "move of savings" and some other problems, thus incurring the collapse of the entire financial system, similar to the financial crisis in Southeast Asia.

Secondly, social corruption is a serious issue. Corruption mainly refers to government officials utilizing their powers to distort justice for a bribe, offering and accepting bribes, the blackmail and extortion of others, conducting power–money deals, spending money extravagantly, and overall becoming dishonest and degenerate. Corruption in China mainly occurs in areas related to price distortion, interference in resource allocation, restrictions on market access, and irrational government control, where the possibility of a huge amount of economic rent and rent-seeking exists. Thus, it is very difficult to control corruption owing to information asymmetry, which provides convenience to corruptors. Compared to corruptions in other fields, the corruptions in the above-mentioned fields play a rather unfortunate influence because of the huge rent in these fields.

Thirdly, problems exist within state-owned enterprises. State-owned enterprises are very important, as they own two-thirds of fixed assets and encompass 60% of urban employment. However, state-owned enterprises have taken a downward turn. Before the reform, state-owned enterprises could earn profits despite the low efficiency, and provide the most revenue tax for the country. After the reform, all methods put forward by economists have been applied (except privatization), but the profit rate has declined continuously.[13]

---

[13] Premier Zhu stated that the state-owned enterprises would work through difficulties within three years, which has been basically completed this year. But how was the goal realized? For example, state-owned enterprises originally had heavy loans in banks and were required to pay interests on the loans, but China adopted "debt-to-equity swap" and therefore they did not have to pay interests. Interests were counted as costs, so no cost existed after the "debt-to-equity swap". Thus, the state-owned enterprises were able to shake off difficulties within three years. However, is the fund cost of the enterprise generally higher for bank loans or for obtaining funds from securities and capital market under general circumstances? Enterprises have three sources of funds, self-funds, and external funds, respectively, including banks and

Fourthly, income gaps exist among different regions. China's economy has grown rapidly after the reform, but the results have not been equally distributed throughout the country. The more rapid economic growth rate in the coastal areas in East China and the relatively backward development in West China have resulted in an increasing regional income gap, thus incurring social and political problems. The peasants from low-income areas migrated voluntarily to high-income areas in search of jobs and this resulted in social problems. In a positive economic status, this migration would provide labor for relatively developed areas, maintain the competitiveness of enterprises, and enable the peasants to send part of their salaries back to their hometowns, which becomes a main capital source for their hometowns. However, in the recent couple of years, few peasants have not been able to find jobs because of slow economic growth. Some of them return to

---

securities market. The self-funds are obviously of the lowest price. How about the cost of the two ways of external funds? Generally, the cost of securities is higher. Why? If I have money, I can choose to save it in a bank or purchase stocks in the stock market. Savings will provide fixed interests without risks, while stocks will provide dividends with risks. The basis of corporation financing includes the risk premium for an asset's investment with risks. Then, the investor will expect a higher average return in stock market than interests obtained from bank savings. The higher returns from the stock market mean a higher cost of the enterprise. Therefore, the "debt-to-equity swap" has covered this problem. The cost of equity is higher than the loan. However, an advantage of stocks lies in the dividends of the stock market. Dividends will be only distributed if the company earns money, compared to bank loans where the companies have to repay due principals and interests. The time constraints for bank loans are fixed, while the time constraints for equity are flexible. The "debt-to-equity swap" did not lower the cost of enterprise financing, but only provided a flexible term for repaying principals and interests. Regarding state-owned enterprises shaking off difficulties within three years, it seems that these enterprises have embraced higher profits than before, but, actually, enterprises have paid a higher cost than bank loans in terms of economic costs. Who will be willing to purchase the stock without returns? Therefore, one of the "Three Stupid Things" in Beijing is "to become stockholders when speculating in shares". State-owned enterprises are really playing an important role. They occupy so many of the country's assets. Will the country be able to burden them if they do not make profits? The "debt-to-equity swap" temporarily avoids payment of interests of dividends distribution, so no one wants the stock. I predict that the stock market will further decline, which shall be finally solved by the government. Does the country have enough money to clear up the mess? The state finance of China occupies a very low proportion of GDP compared to other countries. State-owned enterprises take up 60% urban employment. If they go bankrupt, China will experience severe unemployment and social instability, especially after China joins the WTO.

their hometowns, while others stay at cities without jobs, steady incomes, or places to live, which may become the factor of societal instability. These social problems may also lead to political problems, because East, Central, and Western China may ask for different policies owing to their extremely unbalanced incomes. Eastern China requires market-oriented reform to promote development, while the Western China asks for financial transfer payment.[14] However, the precondition for financial transfer payment is through greater control by the central government, so a conflict is formed. Eastern China hopes for less government control and development according to market laws, but Central and Western China hope that the central government would transfer more from the Eastern China and control more aspects of their governance. The central government can hardly find a policy supported by all areas. The different policy directions of these regions may become the root of political chaos.[15]

The fifth is the environmental problem. Developing countries have all paid some environmental costs in economic development, but China has paid too much.[16] A country's economy cannot grow rapidly if the environment is not suitable for living.

The final problem is the challenge brought by the entry into the WTO. The access to WTO brings many favorable influences to China, such as promoting China's reform by international competition and easing the

---

[14]Deng Xiaoping had divided development into two stages: first, some people and some regions should be allowed to prosper before others, and then, the balanced development of the whole country shall be followed. Later, financial transfer payment to the Central and Western China is also needed.

[15]China will not go into chaos unless the central government is in an uproar. The different policy demands may lead to the disunion of the central government, so the regional income gap must be solved.

[16]Environment is like the health of a person. A person may heal from illnesses and pains without treatments, but, when they seek treatment for a serious condition, it is often too late. Many things have happened in the past 10 years, which really arouse our concerns, such as the three bad floods in the 1990s, each of which was called a-100-year flood. Take the sand storm in 2000 as an example. According to the record, in the recent six or seven centuries, only 70 sand storms have taken place in Beijing, while 40 of them occurred after the foundation of New China and seven of them in 2000. In 2001, the sand storm even appeared on the New Year's Day. Earlier, it had occurred in May or June. If the problem is too severe, it may be too late to fix the environment.

introduction of foreign technologies. However, many still doubt whether China, as a developing country, is well prepared for the challenges brought about by entry to WTO, especially the adaptability of state-owned enterprises.

Each of the above-mentioned problems may lead to the collapse of the Chinese economy when it reaches its development peaks. All countries pay great attention to environmental problems. China can learn from other countries' experiences which would enable it to solve its own economic development problems that would arise.[17] All developing countries also encounter challenges brought on by entrance into WTO. Although China's competitiveness is still not on par with other countries, it cannot enjoy the advantages of globalization without joining in the world mainstream.

Some people believe that China's special national condition and its economic transformation also contributed to its delicate financial system, corruptions, problems in state-owned enterprises, and widening income gap among different regions. The author's opinion is that all these problems are related to state-owned enterprises.

Firstly, why is the proportion of bad bank debts so high? It is because the bank lends the majority of capital to state-owned enterprises. Since state-owned enterprises make small profits, these loans turn into bad debts. Why, then, do banks lend huge capital to state-owned enterprises? It is because these state-owned enterprises will immediately collapse without capital support. In order to solve this problem, the first of the "five reforms" proposed in 1993 was to reform the financial system, which aimed to commercialize banks and liberalize interest rates, i.e., enable the banks to lend money to enterprises who can afford higher interests and run businesses in a favorable way. Then, enterprises can timely repay the loan and the bad debts would be eliminated. But why was the proposal of 1993 not implemented until 2001? It is because no breakthrough was achieved, so

---

[17]Where does the term "The City of Fog", denoting fog in London, come from? It comes from air pollution. This can easily be seen from the impact of air pollution on clothing. For example, 30 years ago, a white shirt worn on the streets of London would turn black after the second day of wear. But London's environment has become much better in recent years. In China, the environmental problem shall be emphasized and a balance between development and environment shall be reached.

state-owned enterprises had to live on the low-interest loans. Therefore, the root of the banking system's problem lies in state-owned enterprises.

Most corruption is embedded in the government regulation. Take the traffic regulations as an example.[18] The treatment method is simple: to raise the salaries of the police and law enforcement officials and heavily punish them if their involvement in any corruption is found. However, the most important reason for widespread corruption in China is the interference of the state in all economic matters. Firstly, the state distorts prices. Since the reform and opening up, the government has increasingly released its control over prices, but, until now, it still controls the bank interest. The current bank interest is much lower than folk debit interest, even by 10%. In an economic aspect, the 10% is the "rent". Interest is not controlled by the market, and a considerable gap exists between the market interest and controlled interest, so the economic interest is called the "rent", since no effort is needed to gain profits, such as with land rent. Whoever controls the cheap capital and raw materials controls the "rent" and can earn huge profits by changing hands. They can also earn money by applying for loans and through transferring money to others. In 1994 and 1995, the total amount of loan reached 4 trillion yuan, so the 10% equaled to 400 billion yuan, which was controlled by several governmental officials and people in the banking systems. Currently, China's bank loan has amounted to 8 trillion yuan each year. If the gap between market interest and official interest is only 5%, the rent is 400 billion yuan. Many people will bribe officials for the sake of the 400 billion yuan. Secondly, the government controls market access. The government controls few industries which are engaged in the market and share great profits owing to their monopoly position. Many people bribe governmental officials to obtain access. Therefore, corruptions in China have already formed a system. Compared with other countries, China suffers more from corruptions because of government's interference in prices and market access.

---

[18] It is a worldwide law to fine any driver that runs a red light. However, if the driver running the red light is caught by the police and fined 200 yuan and two scores deducted from their driving record, the driver may give the police 100 yuan and tell the police not to tell others or report it. The police can earn 100 yuan and the driver can also save 100 yuan. This may be the root of corruption. Another example when the police catch criminals, they may bribe the police with valuable items in exchange for their release. This is also the root of corruption.

Why does the government lower the prices, such as with the loan interest? It is for the existence of state-owned enterprises. Why can the liberation of interest rate not be realized? Why is the rate lowered by an administrative method? It is because state-owned enterprises cannot afford high interest rates,[19] so the interest rate is lowered to protect them. In fact, many unnecessary controls can be released, but they exist for the sake of the hegemony position and profits of state-owned enterprises. In areas where regulations are necessary, the "rent" can be open, licenses can be applied by auction, and the profits shall be incorporated in the state treasury. Through these methods, the "rent" will not become the personal income of governmental officials. Why did the government not follow the above methods? It is because the government needs to let in state-owned enterprises without rent. All these measures are adopted to protect the state-owned enterprises. Why are state-owned enterprises protected? It is because they cannot afford the market price.

It seems that the regional income gap has little relation with state-owned enterprises, but, in fact, the two are closely related. In such a large country as China, different regions are featured with different advantages: the eastern area is more developed, with a higher capital and technology level, and is suitable for manufacturing; the central area is featured with conditions that are favorable for agriculture and agricultural development; and the western area has rich resources and suitable for resource exploration. According to tradition, China always lowers the prices of cotton, grains, and main mineral products in order to guarantee cheap raw materials and the lives of low salaried workers of state-owned enterprises. These are the traditional measures to protect state-owned enterprises. However, after reform and opening up, the development of the manufacturing industry in the eastern area was dependent upon the supply of grains and cotton from the central area and mineral resources from the western area. The lowered prices of produce from the central and western areas indicate the availability of subsidies provided by the central and western areas to the eastern area for development. The increasing gap between the rich and the poor is caused

---

[19]As mentioned above, "debt-to-equity swap" is adopted in the reform on state-owned enterprises, because it is believed that the interest of the loan is a heavy burden. If they cannot afford the current low interest, they can never bear the interest rate after liberalization.

by the poor providing subsidies to the rich. Actually, it is not difficult to find solutions to this problem, such as by releasing the control over the prices. The more developed the eastern area manufacturing industry, the higher the market prices would be for grains and cotton from the central area as well as the prices of natural resources from the western area. In this way, the development of the eastern area would benefit the central and western areas. However, these measures cannot be applied, because state-owned enterprises still need the "hidden" price subsidies.

Therefore, all these problems in the reform seem to be very complicated, including the financial system, corruptions, and regional income gap, but actually are all rooted in state-owned enterprises. In addition to Chinese economists, government officials also understand proper treatment plans to eradicate these problems. Meanwhile, over the last 22 years, the government has been consistently trying to reform the state-owned enterprises where more than half of the measures have been directly related to reforming the state-owned enterprises. However, these efforts have failed.[20] All the measures that were proposed by economists, excluding privatization, have been attempted, including retained earnings, contract system, stock-holding system, and "debt-to-equity swap".

In that case, can privatization solve the problem? In my opinion, privatization cannot be an end to this problem. For example, Russian state-owned enterprises have been privatized, but the problem still remains. What is the fundamental reason for the declining efficiency of state-owned enterprises? At the very beginning, many people believed that factory directors, managers, and workers were not active enough. Therefore, the reform at that time granted power to lower levels and allowed them to keep a bigger share of profits, retain earnings, and carry out the contract system, in the hope that factory directors, managers, and workers would be more motivated to manage better profits for enterprises. However, because no one cared about profits, defects in the property rights appeared as these enterprises were owned by the state. Then, some proposed the property right reform, which advocated a shareholding system. After the reform, the

---

[20]By now, the most successful reform is the rural reform, with the adoption of the household contract responsibility system. However, the surprise is that it is not designed by the government. Most plans of the government in the 21-year reform relate to state-owned enterprises.

property rights should be clearly defined. Some of the shares can be sold to non-state-owned enterprises and individuals, and then these shareholders of non-state-owned enterprises would pay attention to maintaining and increasing the value of assets, which would naturally maintain and increase the value of state-controlled assets. This was a popular opinion at that time, but it failed to find out the root of the state-owned enterprise's problem.

The biggest problem for state-owned enterprises is the heavy policy burden, which leads to policy-related losses. Instead of factory directors and managers, the government is responsible for policy-related losses. The government often provides subsidies or preferential treatment to state-owned enterprises, such as selling raw materials at a low cost and providing low interest loans. Regarding large enterprises, no matter state owned or private, the "separation of the two powers" may result in information asymmetry. The state, as the owner, and the large shareholder of the large enterprise know nothing about how the factory director and manager are managing the enterprise. Under information asymmetry, factory directors and managers may list all losses, including the losses incurred by poor management, under policy-related losses. The owner cannot distinguish policy-related losses and losses incurred by poor management, and therefore, the owner has no other choice but to bear all the losses. If the government is responsible for all these losses, the factory directors and managers may list their own consumptions under these losses or hold meetings in the places of interest. They would justify all losses to policy-related burdens. If the enterprises are well managed, the government may not know the accurate profitability levels, thus enabling the enterprises to transfer large amounts of profits to their own accounts and report losses to the government. Therefore, no reform would succeed if the policy-related burden still exists. Eastern European countries, Russia in particular, have privatized nearly all of their state-owned enterprises, but, according to the research of the World Bank in 1996, these enterprises required more subsidies after privatization. This was because factory leaders and managers were breaking laws when they transferred the subsidies and other preferential inputs into their own accounts, but after privatization, it is legitimate for them to do so, so they require more subsidies and preferential treatment from the government and corruption becomes more prevalent. Therefore, privatization cannot solve this problem, since no reform would work without eliminating policy-related losses.[21] Therefore, the key to this problem is the policy burden.

Policy burdens can be categorized into two types. The first is the strategic policy burden, especially for large state-owned enterprises and capital-intensive industries, and industry sectors. China is a country of relatively scarce resources, so the capital-intensive industries are advantageous to developed countries, but not to developing countries. In a competitive market, no one in the Chinese market is willing to invest in this kind of industry, because it would essentially go bankrupt if it fails in the competition. As a strategic consideration, China had established many enterprises of this kind in the planned economy period and adopted strict, planned control over these enterprises. They were able to survive in that period because all investments came from interest-free state finance. Prices of all input factors were lowered, so the cost was very low. Foreign products could not enter China, so they could gain profits by hegemony in the domestic market. Since the reform and opening up was adopted, these controls have been canceled or are in the process of being canceled. These state-owned enterprises can no longer survive in domestic and foreign competitions. However, the government must be responsible for its investment decisions. This is the strategic policy burden. The second type of policy burden is the social policy burden, which includes two aspects. The first is the redundant enterprise's employee. Before reform and opening up, China invested a great deal in capital-intensive industries and created only a few opportunities. The government was responsible for urban employment, so it often provided employment to urban people.[22] It was not a problem

---

[21] It has been proven by many examples in China. Many listed companies have seen their stocks decline from outstanding stocks to bad stocks over three years when they did not eliminate the policy burden. The author has also conducted some research and found that all companies that have been listed for five years showed the same performance with non-listed companies. Why? They are bearing these policy burdens. Some state-owned enterprises, as well as private enterprises, such as the big companies and consortia in Korea, also bear the policy burden and have very low efficiency as the state-owned enterprises of China do.

[22] The author had a similar experience. When I came back to China in 1979, I was sent to visit and study a big fertilizer plant in Daqing, according to the accepted domestic practices. At the end of the 1970s, China had imported 13 more big fertilizer plants from Romania, each with an output of 300,000 tons. At that time, the factory director told me that only 700 employees were enough for the fertilizer factory of this size according to its original Romanian design, but the Chinese factory had employed 1,500 people because of the employment demand.

before the reform, since all incomes went to the government and government allocated funds to enterprises. The government supported all workers. After the reform and opening up, the burden transferred from the government to enterprises. While state-owned enterprises employed three to four people for a single position, private companies and "triple-funded enterprises" employed one person for a position, bearing a heavier burden. This is not the responsibility of factory directors and managers, but it is the duty of the state. Another kind of social burden is the endowment insurance, medical care, etc. Before the reform and opening, salaries were only used for lifestyle related consumption activities, while endowment and medical care were burdened by state finance. After the reform, these burdens were gradually transferred to enterprises, so the enterprises with more elderly workers had to bear greater levels of burdens. Therefore, state-owned enterprises could not compete with non-state-owned enterprises, which were newer. As the government created these problems, the factory directors and managers had the excuse to require money from the government in order to afford these strategic and social burdens. They could ask for any amount of funds and diverted these into their own accounts. Provided that enterprises always asked for policy preferential from the government, the functions of the government and enterprises became confused. The precondition for the reform on state-owned enterprises is to separate the policy burdens; otherwise, no reform will be effective.[23]

5. Solutions to China's Economic Problems

If the government bears the responsibility for social problems, this will alleviate many problems for workers. Take redundant enterprise employees, for example. It was the government that invested funds in capital-intensive industries and thus incurred the problem, not workers themselves. Redundant employees should be laid off, but the government should

---

When I visited the factory, only one year after its foundation, 2,200 people were employed by the factory.

[23]Take Russia, Eastern Europe, and Korea as examples. Why does the Korean government provide big Korean enterprises with so much preferential treatment and protection? It is to protect the capital-intensive and technology-intensive industries without vitality. This is policy burden. The government has no idea of how much investment is enough, so enterprises can constantly ask for money.

retrain them, arrange jobs for them, and support their basic lifestyle requirements. The retirement insurance is also the government's debt to elderly workers.[24] Currently, the elderly are supported by enterprises. However, the government invested their pensions into other industries. Therefore, an effective social security system should be established, and the endowment insurance for the elderly workers should be separated from enterprises.

The government has enough capital to adopt the above measures, as the current losses of state-owned enterprises would also be borne by the government. Economically, depending on who use the government's money, it would make a great difference. If the government itself uses the money, the enterprise would find no excuse to ask for money. In fact, it would be more economical for the government to spend money by itself, because enterprises would add various fees with the excuse of burden.

For strategic burden, China suffers a higher fund cost owing to scarce resources, and cannot compete with countries of rich funds in this area. This is the main content of the strategic burden. Solutions can be classified into several methods. First, for some products that are necessary for national security and should not be imported from foreign countries, the only way is financial appropriation controlled by the government. Actually, all countries, including developed capitalist countries such as the U.S., adopt the same method for these kinds of products. The second types of products are not necessary for national security but occupy a considerable domestic market. One of the solutions is to establish equity joint venture with developed countries to introduce capitals and technologies, by which China can utilize the low capital cost of developed countries and overcome the disadvantages of fund shortage and high capital cost, while foreign countries can enter China by joint ventures with domestic enterprises, benefiting from China's big market. Another solution is to be directly listed in the foreign capital market, but the preconditions state that the products must occupy a large amount of the domestic market, which also aims to utilize the low cost of international capital and overcome China's

---

[24] According to Marxism, a worker can afford his own living and development demands with his own earnings. The living demands include both his increasing human capital and the education fees of his children.

disadvantages.[25] Then these enterprises would lose their justifications for strategic burden. For the third type of products occupying a small part of the domestic market, the only way is to switch to another product. These enterprises cannot compete with foreign enterprises in capital-intensive industries since the fund cost is too high. However, these enterprises were originally leading enterprises, featured with favorable strengths in many aspects. If they are allowed to switch to another product, they may rely on their advantages in engineering and equipment to switch to products with a large domestic market, which may be more labor intensive.[26] The condition for the switch is a considerable management level, and engineering and design forces. A few state-owned enterprises that do not meet these conditions face bankruptcy, and the government may rearrange their employees. Only very few enterprises belong to the first type necessary for national security, and very few enterprises may go bankrupt. Most state-owned enterprises are featured with certain engineering and management strengths, with or without products occupying a large domestic market. Problems of most state-owned enterprises can be solved by the above solution.[27] After the separation of policy burden, the business operation would become the responsibility of the factory directors and managers. The

---

[25] Actually, the reform in recent years is carried out in this direction. Take the automotive industry as an example. China's automotive companies established joint venture with major foreign carmakers, such as the large automotive factories in Shanghai, Guangzhou, Wuhan, and Changchun, where foreign capital and technologies are introduced. Another example is the production of color films which is more capital intensive, and in China, it is mainly operated based on the joint venture between the entire Chinese industry and the Kodak Company. China Mobile, Chine Telecom, and Sinopec Group, etc., are all listed in foreign markets since they need a great amount of capital.

[26] China has many experiences in this aspect. Sichuan Changhong Group abandoned the original vacuum-tube radar, which shared little market in China and transferred to color television (TV). The production of color TVs, mainly including an assembly process, is labor intensive. It gives full play to China's advantages by utilizing its engineering and design strengths to assemble TVs. In addition to the large domestic market, it even competes with Japanese and Korean companies.

[27] Actually, the 10th Five-Year Plan has incorporated all these policies and measures, but it takes time to implement them. For state-owned enterprises, the biggest difference between the 10th Five-Year Plan and previous reform measures lies in the fact that it clearly indicates an effort to separate the policy burden, though it also proposes the "clearly established ownership".

situation of an irresponsible personnel department would also disappear, because they cannot send anyone they want to the factory as the factory directors and managers would be responsible for the performance of the factory. They would be held accountable if the operation performance is not satisfactory.[28]

In conclusion, many problems related to state-owned enterprises are rooted in the policy burden, while factory directors, managers, and the personnel department have no responsibility for the operation performance. Fortunately, the reform direction has been discovered after a 22-year exploration. Based on this direction, more and more state-owned enterprises would be free of policy burden and become more competitive, based on efficient market management. Of course, it does not necessarily mean that state-owned enterprises would perform well without policy burden. They may succeed, or fail, as other private enterprises do. However, factory directors and managers assume the responsibility of the enterprise's performance, so the directors and managers should be replaced if the state-owned enterprises without policy burden cannot earn profits as expected. State-owned enterprises may also be merged or go bankrupt, but they cannot ask for subsidies from the government. Only in this way can the reform of state-owned enterprises have a chance to succeed. After finding the solution to state-owned enterprises, the direction for the financial system reform becomes clearer, which refers to the marketization of profits and commercialization of banks. Without the protection of state-owned enterprises and support to their hegemony, corruptions may not occur; and

---

[28] Here is a substantive example. After the reform and opening up was adopted, two types of enterprises existed in the foreign trade sector: the old foreign trade sector, of hegemony and responsibility of earning foreign exchange and introduction of technologies, and the new foreign trade companies, without policy burden. However, in old foreign trade companies, it is strange that when managers were sent to other places for work, many people would go to see the leader of the personnel department in the hope of work, but in the new foreign trade companies, they are often not willing to go, even though they are required by the personnel department. This is because, in the old foreign trade companies, they do not need to assume responsibilities, and both managers and the personnel department could make the policy burden an excuse for the bad performance of operation. On the contrary, in new foreign trade companies, managers assume responsibilities for the business performance, and the personnel department cannot send anyone they want, but must choose proper and most qualified persons, otherwise they will also assume the responsibility of sending wrong people to work.

the regional gap difference would gradually disappear, since the increasing demands in developed areas would raise the prices of various products and factors as adjusted by the market, and the development of an area would spur the development of another area.

6. Prospect for the Chinese Economy: Optimistic or Pessimistic

On the one hand, a 30- or 40-year growth potential can be predicted in China based on the introduction of technologies in terms of the technological change. On the other hand, many are skeptical if China, as a developing and transforming country that is joining the WTO, can continue to develop under these current problems. Should an optimistic attitude be held toward Chinese economy? It is important to analyze how these problems are generated and whether China is on the correct path to solving these problems. In reality, problems exist in every period. According to records, societal problems existed in the flourishing age of the Han and Tang Dynasties.[29] The past 22 years can be considered as the "golden years" in Chinese history, though many difficulties appeared each year. Therefore, if we can analyze the origin of these problems, solutions, and whether China is on the correct path to solving their problems, the problems are not insurmountable.

Currently, many problems exist in China, but they are constantly being solved. China would give full play to its development potentials in finding solutions to these problems. Of course, new problems would emerge, but that precisely demonstrates the necessity of economists. Some may feel confident, while others may not under these circumstances. This provides everyone with the opportunity to become "Li Jiacheng" of the mainland.

---

[29] Several days ago, I read an article in the *Selected Ancient Chinese Essays*, which was a reply letter from Li Ling to Su Wu. Li Ling was Li Guang's grandson. Why did he surrender after he was arrested by the Huns? He wrote in the letter that too many treacherous court officials around Emperor Wudi of Han Dynasty suppressed the talent. The novels and TV dramas about emperors at the beginning of the Qing Dynasty have recently become very popular. There is hardly any dynasty better than the Kangxi, Yongzheng, and Qianlong periods in Chinese history, even the Tang and Han Dynasties. However, according to the history novels, people were living a very bad life at that time, while Emperor Yongzheng was carrying many heavy burdens, such as the potential collapse of the country. Every period has its own difficulties. The "flourishing age" is only the retrospection of later generations.

Chapter 2

Economic Development and Chinese Culture*

1. The Cultural Status of Traditional China

A multitude of varying cultures develop from the diverse global landscape, resulting in a unique culture for each country and region. The Chinese, in particular, are very proud of their motherland, which is rich with a long history and splendid culture. China has been recognized as one of the four great ancient civilizations worldwide. Moreover, many domestic and foreign experts believe that Chinese culture and civilization have been the greatest achievements in the world in the 2,000 years before the Industrial Revolution.

Based on the comparison between the eastern and western economic histories, it is generally acknowledged that the Western Han Dynasty and the Roman Empire were relatively even. However, Europe made its passage into the 1,000-year "Dark Ages", compared to China that experienced several flourishing dynasties, including the Han, Tang, Song, Yuan, Ming, and Qing Dynasties.[1]

---

*This chapter was originally published in the *Draft for Discussion of the Chinese Economic Research Center of Beijing University*, 9th issue of 2002, and later published in the *Strategy and Management*, 1st issue 2003.

[1] According to scholars, despite a weak military force, the Song Dynasty made greater achievements than the previous several dynasties in the fields of science, technology, and economics. Yuan Dynasty was the largest empire in Chinese history. Qing established the second largest empire. Qing made great economic and cultural achievements worldwide during the Kangxi, Yongzheng, and Qianlong periods. At the same time, however, Europe suffered poverty and backward agricultural economics. China, with a developed industrial economy, completely led the west. The Scottish social philosopher Adam Smith presented his admiration toward China's economic and cultural accomplishments in his work, *The Wealth of Nations* (1776).

The cultural and economic achievements of China were highly appreciated and worshipped by the west, meanwhile having a profound effect on the surrounding countries and regions. In the famous Kotoku Reformation that took place directly before the Meiji Reformation, Japan promoted the complete study of Tang culture.[2] Chinese culture also deeply influenced the surrounding countries, such as Korea and Thailand.[3]

Before the Industrial Revolution, Chinese culture was regarded as the most developed culture during the previous more than 1,000 years period. Many people made their pilgrimage to China.[4] At the time, in Chinese characters, "English" was added with a character representing the "beast". The European Renaissance that took place before the Industrial Revolution had two main objectives: first, restoring the classical Greek traditions and ancient Greek philosophy in order to be free of the restraints on ideas by medieval theology, and second, studying the people-oriented Confucianism. The study on Chinese culture was also incorporated in the Renaissance. In conclusion, Chinese culture has long been a source of great pride for the Chinese.

2. Efforts in Modernization and Three Levels of Chinese Culture

After the Industrial Revolution, China had ceased to be the world center. This was because of their declining national power, which had suffered the danger of the destruction of the state and nation through oppression by

---

[2]Japan promoted the complete study of Tang culture and sent envoys and students to the Tang Dynasty to learn Chinese culture, similar to China sending students to study abroad after the reform and opening up was adopted in 1978. Therefore, Chang'an could be imagined based on the historical records, or the model of Kyoto, Japan. According to historical documents, the architectural layout of Kyoto copied Chang'an, though its scale was smaller. In addition, Japanese people also read the "Four Books" (*The Great Learning, The Doctrine of Mean, The Analects of Confucius, and The Mencius*) and the "Five Classics" (*Book of Songs, Book of History, Book of Change, Book of Rites,* and *Spring and Autumn Annals*) of China, while their samurai spirit was inspired by the principle theory of Wang Yangming in Ming Dynasty.

[3]Korea had adopted the Confucian and Taoist cultures from China, while Thai people worshipped the same temple god in their palace as the Chinese.

[4]Foreigners were considered barbarians in Chinese people's opinions until the 19th century, and China was regarded as the world center.

western powers, especially after the Opium War. Because of this cultural impact, many people blamed the backward Chinese culture, especially when compared to the western culture. According to mainstream thought around the May Fourth Movement, the Confucian culture was compared to a cannibal hence China should knock down the Confucianism for the revival of China. In their opinions, China's backward culture was reflected by many weaknesses in the behavior of the Chinese people: highly conservative, content with the status quo, their underhanded nature, not seeking thorough understanding of issues, being overly selfish,[5] being extremely tolerant toward vicious powers and social injustice,[6] and being ignorant and boastful. As an integral part of the Chinese culture, the characteristics of the behavior of the Chinese people should be negated by new characteristics based on the current development. The difficulties and backwardness of China were blamed on the culture. Even today, this kind of opinion is deep rooted in the minds of many people. However, many in China believed that it has only grown stronger with cultural changes.

A recent, new ideological trend vigorously advocates the Chinese culture. In addition to Western Europe, North America, Australia, and New Zealand, the emerging industrialized economies in East Asia, Japan, and the "Four Little Dragons" can also be regarded as modern countries. The per-capita income of the Japanese had caught up with and surpassed America in 1988, while the per-capita income in Singapore exceeded America in 1996. The revival of these countries and regions benefited from their rapid economic growth after World War II (WWII). How could these countries and regions stand ahead of other countries and join the group of developed countries that is led by Western Europe and North America? Why do they enjoy such a rapid economic growth? The common

---

[5]Take the famous Chinese saying as an example: "Each one sweeps the snow from his own doorstep and doesn't bother about the frost on his neighbor's roof".

[6]Significant differences can be found between the Chinese and the Jews. In the WWII, China suffered from extremely cruel massacre in Nanjing and lost 20 million lives in the whole war, while 6 million Jews were killed by Germany. Even now, Jews hold deep animosity toward the Nazis involved in the War. However, after the end of WWII, Chiang Kai-shek invited Okamura Yasuji, who had slaughtered many Chinese, as a distinguished guest and even asked for his advice on war tactics, which revealed that the Chinese people were very tolerant with injustice and vicious powers without principles.

factor among these countries and regions lies in the influence of China's Confucian culture. How, then, can the Confucian culture facilitate economic growth? The Confucian culture has actually contributed a great deal to their economies in catching up with the most developed western countries, as the deciding factor. It is because the Confucian culture emphasizes hard work, thriftiness, assiduity, knowledge,[7] appropriate formalities between the young and old,[8] and importance of faith among friends.[9] Therefore, China owes its success to the advantages of the Confucian culture.

This situation is similar the western countries. Max Weber believed that Christianity and Protestant ethics are directly related to the rise of capitalism.[10] Much focus has been laid in identifying those aspects of the Confucian culture that were actually embedded in the economic development of Eastern Asia, including China. Since the May Fourth Movement, not only did the Chinese intellectuals criticize the Confucian culture and advocated to fight against Confucianism but also other regions that were initially influenced by the Confucian culture blamed it.[11] However, as the economy grew, they now owe the economic revival to the advantages of the Confucian culture.

What is the role of the Confucian culture, the obstacle in the economic development of this region, or the basis for the economic development? Whose saying is right? Or, are they both right, or are they both wrong? How should the Chinese view Chinese culture, especially the traditional culture? These are the topics to be discussed in this chapter.

Before the role of the Chinese culture is discussed, the definition of culture should be clarified first. Different scholars have different definitions of the culture, and the author accepts the definition of culture from

---

[7]"To be a scholar is to be at the top of the society." The emphasis on knowledge exactly accords to the age of knowledge economy.

[8]The society is stable and in good order, instead of being in chaos.

[9]The faith and credit emphasized by the Confucian culture meets the requirements of modern commercial civilization.

[10]Max Weber was a German sociologist. He explained the rise of capitalism in western countries based on the Protestant ethic in his influential work, *The Protestant Ethic and the Spirit of Capitalism.*

[11]For example, I grew up in Taiwan. The Confucian culture was the first thing to be blamed in criticizing the backwardness of China, mainly directed at the lack of scientific spirit, sluggish development, etc.

Fei Xiaotong.[12] He believes that culture includes three levels. The first level refers to tools utilized by the state for production and living. For example, the Chinese use chopsticks, westerners use forks, and Indians use their hands to consume food. In addition, different countries may use different tools to fight the war, such as firearms or swords and spears. The second level is the level of organization. According to Fei Xiaotong, this refers to how the society organizes individuals to socialize together, live together, and interact with each other, such as in a political organization, religious organization, production organization, and the state apparatus. The third level is the value. How do people think? What can they accept or not accept? What is good? What is bad? Different societies share different values on good and bad and different standards for behaviors and opinions.[13] The three levels together form an integrated approach.

For example, in primitive society, spears and arrows were applied as the production and living tools in the New and Old Stone Ages, with spearheads and arrowheads made of stone. In terms of social organization, primitive society shared an equal social organization, where, under the leadership of one person, other people basically shared equal status, while only a few were divided to be warriors and hunters, very different from the modern organization. In terms of values, there was no distinction between "you" and "me" on the ownership of many things,[14] but in modern society, things only belong to their owners.[15] Ethnology scholars mainly recorded the tools, organization methods, and values of primitive society in their inspection of primitive society, which may vary between different societies, places, or historical stages and form an integral part. Take the market as an example. In primitive society, people left their excessive food and clothes by the wayside, which could be taken by the passers-by, only if they left something there

---

[12]Fei Xiaotong made an excellent presentation on the theory on three factors of culture from Malinowski in his translation of the *Theory on Culture*, Commercial Press, 1946.

[13]For example, Song Jiang is a good man as he let go of the criminal and became the leader of the LiangShan Marsh, but in most Americans' opinions, a person who lets go of a criminal is a bad man.

[14]For example, when a hunter went hunting and returned with his kill, all people of the community would share. However, if a hunter failed to catch anything, he could still share the kill brought back by other hunters.

[15]If I eat things at your home without your consent, you can have the police arrest me under the accusation of theft. It is very different in primitive society.

in exchange. The owner would then witness who took his castaways and who left things behind. This is an organization style. However, in modern society, one can never take the belongings of others else they will be arrested for theft. In primitive society, according to their values, anyone who took things away without leaving something in exchange could be caught and punished, no matter how far they had traveled. In modern society, anyone who takes things away would be arrested, but the attack or assassination of individuals is not allowed, otherwise they would also be arrested. Therefore, culture varies in different societies and different historical stages, including differences in artifacts, organization styles, and behavioral norms. Without external interference, the culture self-sustains, while its production tools, social organization methods, and values are also self-consistent.

Based on this definition, in the observation of the historical evolutions in modern China, it is easy to understand many social and political movements and divide them into stages. Before the Industrial Revolution, in addition to the Chinese, Adam Smith also recognized Chinese culture as a leader to the western culture in all directions. However, since the Opium War, China has lost many wars. What happened to China? Why did the country that had led the world for almost 2,000 years suffer such repeated defeats? Many people, especially Chinese scholars, who took the responsibility to answer these questions about the fate of the country, had carefully researched these questions. Their thoughts were necessary to make China stronger in the face of the risks of the destruction of the country and nation. The earliest opinion considered that the Confucian culture played an important role in attaching appropriate formalities between the emperor and ministers, fathers and sons, and the young and the old to be good; and the main cause for China's defeat was the backwardness in firearms and warships. The cultural opinion was to develop a unique cultural ideology, "guided by traditional Chinese values and aided with modern western values". Under the guidance of this idea, the "Westernization Movement" was initiated by Zeng Guofan, Li Hongzhang, and Zuo Zongtang, among others, and lasted for 30 years, when they bought the most advanced weapons of the world. The Movement was halted until the Sino-Japanese War of 1894–1895 broke out. Before the War, Chinese and many foreigners believed that China would win, because the Beiyang Fleet of China ranked fifth in the world in terms of the tonnage and owned the most advanced large ships and weapons. By comparison, Japan had carried out the Meiji Restoration at the same time after the closed-door policy of Japan was forced to be abandoned, because of America's attack, under the leadership of Admiral Perry. Before the Sino-Japanese War of 1894–1895, Japan's ships were smaller and less advanced than China's since they were made by the Japanese themselves, so many Chinese and foreign commentators considered that China would definitely win.[16] However, it turned out that China was defeated by Japan.

The Sino-Japanese War of 1894–1895 was a great shock to the Chinese. Japan had been a young apprentice of China for more than 1,000 years. The Japanese introduced Chinese culture, sent their students to China to learn, and brought the best things and classics of China back to Japan for study. How could they defeat China? Chinese people reflected that, in addition to the advanced weapons and production tools, other things were needed to make China stronger. It was noticed that Japan had become much stronger in only two or three decades after the Meiji Restoration, because it had carried out a thorough and complete reform and learned the western systems besides their firearms. After the Meiji Restoration, politically, Japan confirmed the constitutional monarchy and the majority party formed the cabinet in the parliament; militarily, they invited German drill masters on land forces to reform Japanese armies and transferred the leadership of the armies from the local royalties to the state government; In education, they promoted the western style of compulsory education; and economically, introduced the banking and enterprises systems from the west. Therefore, the Chinese began to realize that the reform on the organization level was necessary, in addition to the artifacts level, such as firearms. Two different schools co-existed at that time: the school of the constitutional monarchy headed by Kang Youwei and Liang Qichao, who advocated to carry out the reform similar to the Meiji Restoration of Japan and adopted modern political, economic, social, and educational

---

[16] According to the unofficial historical record, before the War, China had held a review of troops by Huangpu River in Shanghai in order to let Japan quit after learning of the difficulties involved. China had invited foreign military officials stationed in China and showed the most advanced navy. Japan was very cautious and sent a military official stationed in China at that time to the review. However, after the review of troops, the Japanese official reported to their prime minister that he believed that Japan could defeat China despite their weaker weapons. He said in the review that he found the weapons advanced and soldiers valiant, but he found Chinese sailors on some other naval vessels to be unorganized and immature, so a troop without order or modern spirit would definitely fail.

systems, under the basic framework of the Qing Dynasty; and the bourgeois revolution led by Sun Zhongshan, who believed that the reform at the level of the social organization under the rule of Qing Dynasty was not enough and it was necessary to overthrow the Qing Dynasty and study the system of separation of powers from America, as well as other economic, social, and educational systems.[17] Finally, the democratic bourgeois revolution under the leadership of Sun Zhongshan overthrew the Qing government. Chinese scholars and common people at that time shared similar ideas with intellectuals and community leaders of the Soviet Union and the Eastern Europe.[18] Although they had a deeper understanding compared to the "Westernization Movement" and paid attention to the reform of social organizations in addition to the firearms, China did not get stronger right away.[19]

The May Fourth Movement had gone deeper into the third level of thinking. As a New Culture Movement, the May Fourth Movement realized that, in addition to the new learning on politics, such as the constitution, president, parliament, or the establishment of Beijing University, as well as the modern army, further reforms related to culture should be carried out at a deeper level, so they proposed democracy and science. It was related to values, ethical concepts, and the criteria of right and wrong. According to the Movement, China could only get stronger based on democracy and science.

In conclusion, China had experienced a deepening three-level of understanding on why China that was originally a celestial country became a poor developing country of the world, in terms of Chinese culture.

---

[17] Wu Hsu Reform was soon repressed by the Empress Dowager. One of the few, or maybe the only, achievement of the Reform was the establishment of Beijing University. After the Boxer Uprising, Empress Dowager came to realize that reform was the only choice. She transformed the system of six boards to the modern parliament system and carried out reform in education systems and other areas, but it was too late.

[18] Currently, many people in the Soviet Union and Eastern Europe consider the Communist party and socialist system as the evil spirit and believe that they could lead their lives as Western Europeans and Americans, once they overthrow the Communist party and cancel the socialist system. Similarly, at that time, the Chinese felt that China could become strong once the Qing government had been overthrown.

[19] Although China was the victorious nation in WWI, after the victory, Qingdao, the concession was only transferred to Japan from Germany, but had not been returned to China.

3. Economic Development and Cultural Changes

Compared to the west, China had realized its own backwardness in the level of tools, level of organizations, and also in the level of spirit and values. How would China rise again? Two different theories could be referred to on this matter. The first kind of theory, with Max Weber as the representative, showed great influence on the west, as well as the two or three generations after the May Fourth Movement. Why were most developed countries capitalist economies before the 1930s? How did these Western European and North American countries become capitalist countries and grow strong? A certain relationship was found between the capitalism and the richness of a country. Why did capitalism emerge? According to Max Weber, Calvinist doctrines proposed the idea of emphasis on saving, engagement in production, and expansion of reproduction and regarded these traits as standard behavior. The standard was then widely accepted by Protestants, who started to attach importance to modern life and the current life instead of the afterlife. The change in ethnics and values laid the foundation for future capitalism and Industrial Revolution. According to his opinion, the ethical values of China indeed disagreed with the modern spirit, such as the reflections on the Confucian culture in the May Fourth Movement, and proposed that China should invite "democracy and science" as proposed in the May Fourth Movement, that is to say become totally westernized. This idea has showed huge influence on the Chinese scholars until now.[20]

This theory was self-consistent, but it was not practical. Where does everyone's values come from? Values are not innate, but are learned when people are young.[21] Therefore, even though the Chinese accept Max

---

[20]The most obvious example was the TV series *River Elegy* in the late 1980s, which discussed the modernization of China and the reason for the prosperity in ancient times and the decline in modern times. It proposed the "yellow culture" and "blue culture". The yellow culture developed in Loess Plateau of China, as a conservative, backward, and agriculture-oriented civilization, while the blue culture of the west represents an ocean culture, symbolizing the conquest of the nature. The opinion of the *River Elegy* actually inherited the opinions of the May Fourth Movement, which indicated that China should change the overall culture in order to become stronger. In addition to the satellites, atom bombs, and modern organizations, China should establish a modern spirit, similar to the west.

[21]A famous Chinese saying states that "the childhood shows the man", which has been demonstrated by psychological studies. The behaviors and values of a person have been

Weber's opinion and believe that it is necessary to change values firstly, or the Chinese should westernize themselves and accept western values and ethnics in an all-around way, these are difficult to implement. Chinese people are growing in the Chinese society and cannot completely rid themselves of Chinese ethnicities and values or accept those from the west. According to this theory, China can hardly get strong.

Another theory actually refers to Marx's theory, which states that culture includes three different levels: artifacts, organization, and spirit. Among the three levels, artifacts, i.e., the production tools, refer to the economic basis that decides the superstructure. Any change of the economic basis will lead to the change of the superstructure. According to Max Weber, the super-structure decides the economic basis, compared to Marxism that believes the economic basis decides the superstructure. The author is disposed to agree with the latter opinion, i.e., the economic basis decides the superstructure.[22]

For example, the primitive communistic society emphasized mutual cooperation, with common ownership and common production as their value. The formation of values is related to the economic basis. At that time, the production tool was very primitive. How about the methods of production? In the primitive nomadic hunting society, beasts ran faster and were stronger than people, so people could only hunt the beasts upon organization. Therefore, the society of common production and sharing[23] was formed. The principle of sharing was significantly related to the

---

finalized before the age of seven. Everyone learns to distinguish right from wrong, that they were rewarded for the right and punished for the wrong in their interactions with parents, siblings, friends, and neighbors since birth, so their ideas have been formed from childhood. For example, based on our observations, the sayings, behaviors, and concerns of Yang Zhenning and Li Zhendao are in accordance with the Chinese values.

[22]Under a stable situation without external forces, a culture should be a self-consistent system. Under the external forces, competition, and rapid changes, especially when the productivity is not spontaneous, based on the economic basis, some aspects of the self-consistent approach would develop faster, while others would develop slower, thus leading to many conflicts. In terms of the process of historical development, the level of artifacts is the first to be discovered and the easiest to be learned; the next is the level of organization; and the third is the level of spirit, which cannot be learned or compulsively added, but adjustments in minds are needed. Therefore, a change in the economic basis would lead to a change in the superstructure.

[23]In the primitive society, some may engage in hunting as an individual, or in a group. Some might catch prey, while others might not. After they have caught prey, they would eat it. They could not store the excess meat if they could not eat it all, so it was better to give it to

productivity. Along with the development of productivity, society had transformed from a nomadic hunting to a farming society. Compare the two different societies. Firstly, the productivity of the agricultural society is more stable. Despite the influence of the climate, the time and amount of the planting output could be estimated, compared to the inability to predict hunting results. The production could reach the expectation based on the production tools and methods in the agricultural society. Secondly, the products could be better reserved, and the grains could be restored for the next year after drying. Therefore, it was not necessary to maintain the social habit of sharing. The production organization had transformed from communities to families. The wealth was divided in order to improve the production efficiencies. In addition, the market system had also changed.[24]

In the long process of the historical development, the superstructure, social organization, and values have been constantly changing along with the development of productivity, in terms of the culture. When two different cultures, one of higher productivity and one of lower productivity, collide with each other, how will the culture of lower productivity develop? Here, two problems in different levels will be raised: how will the productivity and the superstructure develop? Firstly, since the superstructure is dependent on productivity, an improvement in the overall cultural level is necessary especially when the declining culture is challenged by the powerful culture. The main problem is how to raise the productivity level. Secondly, after the productivity has been improved, the question is whether the superstructure is able to constantly adjust and enrich itself along with the development of productivity. The two problems should be studied in parallel to further research Chinese culture and Chinese economic development. Is there any method to rapidly develop Chinese productivity? Can the superstructure of

---

others. Therefore, if they could not catch prey the next time, they could accept food from others. They could share the risk in this way.

[24]In the primitive society, people put excessive things by the wayside, because the market was not needed based on such a low productivity. Why did people hide behind a tree, instead of by their discarded things after they put them by the wayside? It was because passers-by did not know whether anyone was there or not. If the person was required to stand by their things, a labor was wasted. What was the reason for chasing down and punishing someone who took something without putting something back? It was because no one would leave things by wayside without this principle.

the Chinese culture be constantly adjusted along with the improvement of the productivity, especially in the level of spirit?[25]

4. Economic Development and the Future of Chinese Culture

The future of China's economic development in the 21st century is estimated to be optimistic in terms of productivity. In the study of the economic development and productivity level of the country and society, three aspects shall be taken into consideration. The first is the possibility of an increase in the three factors, including land, labor, and capital. The most important is, evidently, the increase in capital, since the land generally sees no increase; the labor is limited and only the capital can grow at a rapid rate. The second aspect is the production structure. The factors should be transferred from the low-value and low-productivity products and industries to the products and industries of higher added value, leading to economic growth. The third is technology. Based on the given factors and production structure, improvements in technologies would facilitate the development of productivity.

The most important among the three is the possibility of technological innovation, because the first two sources depend on technological innovation. Capital accumulation would incur decreasing investment return and lower capital return without technological innovation. A high capital accumulation can only be realized based on the rapid technological innovation. Regarding the structure innovation, new products and industries of higher added value would not emerge without new technologies. For example, the information industry of high added value is the result of a new information technology. The high added value is the result of technological innovation. Under these circumstances, the possibility of the structure innovation depends on the potential of technological innovation. Therefore, it is only necessary to figure out the possibility of technological innovation of the country and society to judge the economic development or the productivity of the country. The definition of technological innovation varies in different countries and development stages. In most developed

---

[25]The level of organization is not difficult to learn, since it can be directly copied from the western constitution. The superstructure includes organization, spirit, etc.

countries, technological innovation equals to technological invention, i.e., research and development (R&D), which is high in cost. For developing countries, in addition to the invention, technological imitation can be utilized for technological innovation, because they can utilize their technological gap with developed countries and imitate their advanced technologies. Technological innovation refers to a newer technology in the next production activity, but does not necessarily mean the latest technology. In conclusion, the only way for developed countries to realize technological innovation is invention, while developing countries can select invention or introduction. The cost is an important factor contributing to developing countries' selection from the two methods. Which method costs less? R&D on most sophisticated technologies are very expensive. Currently, the information industry is the hottest industry. In 2000, IBM's investment on R&D was US$4.345 billion,[26] Intel invested US$3.897 billion,[27] and Motorola invested US$4.437 billion.[28] At the same time, the success ratio of investment was low. According to some studies, on average, only 5 out of 100 researches succeed. Once successful, a patent can be applied for the researched new technology and win a protection period of 20 years. However, a technology that obtains a patent is not necessarily valuable, because the products produced by this technology may not be welcomed by consumers, or the cost of the products may be far beyond the purchasing capacity of consumers. According to researches, only one or two technologies out of 10 technologies with patents have commercial value. Of course, the return on a successful technology is very high, amounting to 1 or 2 billion yuan or even more. However, when 99% failure rate is taken into consideration, the return rate on the most sophisticated technologies is not high. It needs US$5 billion to compete with IBM, which cannot be afforded even by the government. The total budget of the Chinese government is only 600 or 700 billion yuan, i.e., less than US$100 billion, which only equals to the investment of 20 enterprises, similar to IBM. China cannot afford the investment on the research of the most sophisticated technologies. The other method is the introduction of technologies, which is generally much lower than invention. The protection of a technology lasts for 20 years at most,

---

[26] www.ibm.com/flat/fncl/3-5-18-fncl-notes.html

[27] www.intel.com/intel/annual00/f-sumary.htm

[28] www.prolytix.com/mot/table2.html

according to the patent. No cost will be paid for the use of the technology after 20 years. It does not even cost much to introduce the technology within 29 years because only one-third of the cost of the invention of the technology is enough for introduction. Meanwhile, the introduced technologies are necessarily successful with commercial values. Therefore, as a developing country, the introduction of technologies would facilitate the technological innovation. The introduction of technologies can be rapid, comprehensive, and in large amounts owing to the low cost, so developing countries can see a wider and quicker technological innovation than developed countries based on the introduction of technologies, and therefore, may develop at rapid speed than the developed countries. Many people are analyzing the reason for the miraculous development of Japan and Asian's "Four Little Dragons". The most important reason is that they realized their technological gap with developed countries and attained a rapid economic growth through the introduction of technologies. Why was the rate of economic growth of China faster after the reform and opening up? The biggest difference is that China had paid much cost on the most sophisticated technology and tried to stand on its own feet to catch up and surpass other countries in technologies, compared to the dependence on the introduction of technologies after the reform and opening up, which led to a much faster economic development.

It is obvious to all that China has experienced rapid economic development in the past two decades. How will China's economic development be in the next three or four decades, or even in the next one or two centuries? The author is very confident about a positive development. It is believed that China can at least maintain an economic growth at 8% to 10% (similar to the past 20 years) in the next three decades, according to analogy. Japan had maintained a rapid economic growth in the 40 years between WWII to the late 1980s; and Asia's "Four Little Dragons" had also maintained a rapid 40-year economic growth since the late 1950s to the start of the financial crisis. Similar to these countries, which mainly relied on the introduction of technologies, it is expected that China would maintain a rapid economic growth for 40 years. In addition, the author believes that China can maintain growth for at least 50 years. Unrelated to the intelligence, it is mainly because the technological gap between China and developed countries in 1979, when China started to promote economic development through the introduction of technologies, was larger than the technological gap of Japan in 1950 and Asia's "Four Little Dragons" in the late 1950s and early 1960s to developed countries. Based on the above calculations, if China maintains the development rate it had in the past 20 years, then during the next 39 years, China would catch up with America by 2030 in the economic scale, but the per-capita income would remain about one-fifth of America as China's population is five times greater than that of America. Since the per-capita income is the indicator for the measurement of the technological level of a country, the technological gap between China and developed countries would still be large in 2030, so it is still possible for China to utilize the technological gap and promote economic development by the introduction of advanced technologies. Will China always fall behind developed countries based on technological introduction? The answer is no. Japan and Singapore depended on the introduction of technologies, but their per-capita incomes have succeeded America.

Two questions have often been raised when the idea of promoting economic development by the introduction of technologies is advocated. Firstly, does it mean that developing countries do not need R&D at all? Secondly, as China facilitates economic development through the introduction of technologies, fewer technologies can be introduced along with increasingly higher economic development levels and narrowing the gap of per-capita incomes to developed countries, rather than when China has to invent technologies. However, since China has been introducing technologies for a long time, will it lose its ability in invention and creation?

For the first question, developing countries can also conduct R&D in addition to the introduction of technologies. A new technology introduced by an enterprise can be compatible with the currently available technologies of the enterprise, which may lead to changes in both the new and old technologies. It is essentially a kind of invention and innovation. In addition, constant improvements shall be conducted on the currently available technologies during the process of production, resulting in many minor and process patents. An enterprise that constantly carries out technological improvements would definitely be more competitive than the enterprise with fewer technological improvements under the same conditions. However, except for the national defense, developing countries should not become involved in the R&D of most sophisticated technologies and products of huge investment and great risks. In fact, R&D can be considered as an industry, which can be divided into different sectors according to the intensity of capital investment, similar to common industries. Developing countries should select sectors where they can show their advantages in terms of the factor endowment.

Many people are concerned about the second problem, because they foresee a sea of troubles in Japan's current economic development despite its rapid economic growth before the 1980s. Some scholars link it to the weaker innovation ability of Japanese than the Americans. The author thinks that it is not necessary to be concerned with this question. There are three most important deciding factors for the invention of the most sophisticated technologies. The first factor is the investment. The theory for the invention of the most sophisticated technologies is very simple.[29] However, most efforts to turn the fundamental and well-known science to new technologies are put on trials which are very expensive. Similar to the purchase of lottery tickets, the more you invest, the higher would be your success ratio.[30] China has to invent the most sophisticated technologies until China's per-capita incomes catch up with America. This is because China's economic scale is five times that of America and China contributes five times that of America's investment on the R&D of most sophisticated technologies, so the success rate of China is five times that of America. Of course, in addition to the monetary gains, China needs scientists to conduct scientific research. The abilities of scientists to conduct research come from both connate abilities and previous studies. Conducting research based on previous studies is simple, and shows no big difference among people. The most important is the connate ability. The cleverer the scientists are, the bigger would be the success rate. China's population is five times that of America and so the talents of the Chinese are also five times that of America. Based on the five times of America's investment and five times of America's talents, the success rate of China is 25 times that of America. Japan is currently competing with America. Why is it so hard for Japan?

---

[29]The principle of superconduction and computer chip and the switch of "zero and one" formed upon the combination of capacitance and electric resistance are utilized in the operation, which is taught in universities.

[30]If the rate of winning the prize with one lottery ticket is about 1%, then the rate would increase 100 times more by buying 100 tickets.

It is because Japan's economic scale and populations are only half of that of America. In addition, Japan is a comparatively closer society. America relies on Chinese talents and worldwide talents, while Japan relies only on its own talents, so Japan fails in the competition. However, China has more talents than America and can also open the door of the country and invite foreign talents to China in the future. The third deciding factor is the standard of the most sophisticated technologies. Standards are very important in the most sophisticated technologies. It is very difficult to tell which standard is better, but the products that are based only on the most sophisticated technologies can be competitive on a larger scale and lower cost. When China's per-capita income catches up with America, China's economic and market scales would be five times that of America, as China's population is five times that of America. Since Japan's market scale is only half of America, Japan is placed at a disadvantage and can only follow America's standards. However, China's market scale would be five times that of America, so America would have to follow China.

Therefore, in view of productivity, China should mainly rely on the introduction of technologies especially when its technological gap to developed countries is comparatively large. China would give play to its advantage of large population when the gap of technologies, i.e., the economic gap, has been narrowed. The Chinese can be optimistic and pay attention that the superstructure must accord to the productivity.

The economic basis has been discussed above. According to Marxism, there is another principle on the relation between the superstructure and economic basis. If the superstructure does not change along with the economic basis, it will inhibit the development of productivity in reverse. China's prospect is optimistic, based on the possibility of the development of productivity. However, can China's Confucianism-based superstructure and cultural traditions advance with the times? Will China's cultural traditions become the burden for economic development? To answer this question, the analysis on whether China's Confucian culture is conservative is needed. Confucius, as the representative of Confucianism, is often considered to be conservative, because he merely explained and discussed on others' theories, but did not write his own theories[31] and mentioned "three sage

---

[31] *Confucian Analects, Shu Er.*

kings" and "five virtuous emperors of China at the dawn of human civilization" at any time. Does this mean that he only sorted out the classics and systems at the period of three sage kings and five virtuous emperors, but did not innovate anything? The author believes that is not so. Why is Confucius praised so highly? Confucius reflected the spirit of that age.[32] Although he only explained others' theories, he selectively sorted out these theories according to the needs of the age, instead of directly copying the ancient ideas, so as to reflect the spirit of the age. He was recognized as the philosopher of the period since he was not conservative. He practically analyzed what was needed in the society and advocated the organization form and ethnics that can promote social development according to the demand of the age. Similar to Confucius, other Confucian masters were also not conservative. For example, Wen Tianxiang had summarized the Confucian philosophy as that "Confucius advocated for humaneness and Mencius advocated for righteousness, while righteousness can only be realized based on humaneness". Humaneness is the core of Confucius's philosophic thinking, while righteousness is the representative of Mencius's philosophic thinking. Humaneness and righteousness share many common grounds, but also see differences. What is humaneness? Confucius mentioned humaneness in more than 20 places in the Confucian Analects, such as "humaneness refers to the interpersonal relations".[33] Humaneness means to treat others like one treats oneself, as Confucius stated that "do not do to others what you do not want others to do to you"[34] and man should help others to be successful in addition to his own success.[35] Humaneness refers to the treatment of the world and society according to one's heart. Then, what is righteousness? Righteousness is different from humaneness and refers to suitability. Humaneness is the way to live, while righteousness is the way to develop.[36] Righteousness has different meanings in different ages and different societies. Mencius said that there are some things a man should and should not do.[37] He also stated that, upon

---

[32] *The Works of Mencius, First Half of Wang Zhang's Statements.*

[33] *The Works of Mencius, Second Half of Wang Zhang's Statements.*

[34] *Confucian Analects, Yan Yuan; Confucian Analects, Weiling Gong.*

[35] *Confucian Analects, Yung.*

[36] *The Works of Mencius, First Half of Li Lou's Statements.*

[37] *The Works of Mencius, Second Half of Li Lou's Statements.*

reflection, one should stick to what he was doing against the opposition of the world if he found that a particular thing was beneficial to the society.[38] Confucianism developed a principle theory in the Song and Ming Dynasties, which was formed based on the attack by Buddhist philosophy and the social progress. The original Confucian philosophy has not fully solved the problems that were brought about by social development. Zhu Xi's principle theory is different to the primary meaning of Confucius and Mencius's theories, as he advocated pursuing the very source of learning.[39] It means to analyze the principle of a particular matter by observation in order to attain knowledge. Later, Wang Yangming, another representative of the principle theory, advocated to implement things "in good conscience".[40] He believed that the criterion for what is good or bad was inside one's heart, so he advocated being free of what inhibits the conscience, thus restoring the conscience. It can be seen that Confucianism has been renewed by scholars of different ages in its history for more than 2,000 years. Since Confucius, its content reflected the demands of the age. The Confucian philosophy could constantly develop along with the change of economic basis, expand the superstructure, and ensure the unanimity between the superstructure and economic basis. This is why the Eastern Asian economy could catch up with the west in the 20th century.

According to Max Weber, modernization can only be realized upon "complete westernization", which means that the Chinese should fully accept western values. However, Japan and Asia's "Four Little Dragons" did not do so. They had retained many of their traditional values. For example, the Japanese continues to attach importance to the authority, a great difference with western spirit. America and Europe emphasize on innovation, but think little of the sense of hierarchy. Japan and South Korea have realized modernization in this way. Based on the huge potential for the development of productivity, the Chinese should be aware that the superstructure would be constantly adjusted to meet the development of productivity. The Chinese should give priority to the development of

---

[38] *The Works of Mencius, First Half of Gongsun Chou's Statements.*

[39] According to Zhu Xi, the "fate" of each particular is constituted with the natural endowment in the "principle" and "Qi", and the "fate decreed by Heaven" should be sought.

[40] The "conscience" refers to the expansion of inborn knowledge, moral consciousness, conscience, or intuition, while the conscience is the original consciousness.

productivity. In addition, the Chinese should believe that the culture and way of action would change along with variations in the economic basis. Some of the previous beliefs should be renounced in the change, but at the same time, China should not simply copy the west. When China's economy becomes the most powerful in the world, China's culture would become the most admirable culture, because the economic basis decides the superstructure. For example, discussing American culture in the 19th century, or saying that American culture will invade Chinese culture at the beginning of 20th century was a laughable topic, but today, many people are concerned about the invasion of American culture. It is because in the process of the development of economic strength of America, its culture has gradually adapted to its powerful economy in terms of organizations and values. For example, McDonald's emergence has saved time in the modern, busy American lifestyle. Therefore, along with the economic development, Chinese culture would also develop based on Chinese traditional culture in terms of artifacts, organizations, and values.

To catch up with the west, China should surpass the west in the level of artifacts and organizations (the political, social, and trade organizations would increasingly converge), but meanwhile keep the unique Chinese-style characteristics. Similar to France, Germany, Italy, and Great Britain, China does not need to be "completely westernized". What would be the unique characteristics of the Chinese culture? It is impossible to foretell, but they would be selected by social competition. As a scholar, the author wants to state that traditional Chinese culture has reached a high civilization stage, and the author sees huge potential in the development of artifacts and productivity and knows that the superstructure would adjust along with the development of productivity and react upon the economic basis. In view of this historical development, China's superstructure of traditional culture has been constantly changing. Based on the experiences of East Asia, the Chinese culture can adapt to the economic basis of modern productivity. What would the Chinese culture be? The answer would be found then. However, I know that along with the revival of Chinese economy in the world, the position of the Chinese culture would be restored.

Chapter 3

The Revival of China and the Future of Chinese Entrepreneurs*

The term "Chinese entrepreneurs" refers to a special group of people who share a strong sense of national identity; the blood of the Chinese nation, no matter whether they are living at home or abroad, connects them. Based on the economic foundation laid by their grandparents or parents through a lifetime of effort, the new dynamic generation of young Chinese entrepreneurs takes over the family business, or makes a new start to seek out new opportunities.

More importance shall be attached to Chinese entrepreneurs, especially the young generation and those who start businesses overseas.

1. Chinese Entrepreneurs Overseas

Currently, many Chinese entrepreneurs are running enterprises overseas. The proportion of economic contributions made by Chinese entrepreneurs in some countries and regions is much higher than the proportion of the Chinese population, especially in Southeast Asian countries. For example, in Indonesia, the Chinese make up only 3% of the local population, but contribute to more than 50% of the local economic development, much like the situation in Malaysia, the Philippines, and Thailand.

Why do so many Chinese entrepreneurs do business overseas? The author considers an important cause to be the vast population and limited farmland of China. In particular, on the southeast coast of China, the heavy burden on population forced many people to migrate overseas. China's long history, glorious culture, advanced political, economic, and social

---

*This is the address to the opening ceremony of the First Young Chinese Merchants Summit held in Beijing on January 7, 2005.

organizations, along with families' high regard for education provides them with a strong ability for social organization, a capacity to adapt to their new environment, and evident advantages in social and human capitals compared to natives that are comparatively backward in economic, cultural, and social development. However, settlers generally controlled these countries politically and while the white people showed advantages in the culture, the overseas Chinese could hardly participate. After World War II (WWII) and subsequent independence of their countries, the natives secured political power to rule. The overseas Chinese can only effectively use their advantages in human and social capitals to develop commerce, and actively participate in economic activities by developing the local market, meanwhile, utilizing the special natural resources that are available locally. Overseas Chinese have attracted much attention in the comparatively backward regions in Southeast Asia, but showed relatively smaller economic and political influences among more politically and economically developed European and American countries.

No matter where the overseas Chinese are and how great an influence they exert, they share a common ground — their national identity. Such people have been educated with Confucian culture, which attaches great importance sustaining family values with the ancestral home and motherland. Overseas Chinese greatly supported Sun Zhongshan during the Chinese revolution. He stated that "Overseas Chinese gave the birth to revolution". This was reiterated by the fact that most foreign capital attracted by China during its reform and opening up in 1978 to the mid-1990s came from overseas Chinese entrepreneurs. Some foreign economists believe that the capital support by overseas Chinese was the main reason for the success of China's gradual reform process. This saying is not quite correct, because the foreign capital only accounted for less than 5% of the total investment on China's fixed assets before 1992, whereas Chinese economy had maintained a growth rate of 9% on average from 1978 to 1992. However, the direct foreign investment had greatly contributed to China's economic growth.

2. Challenges and Opportunities for Chinese Entrepreneurs

Chinese entrepreneurs face some challenges. Firstly, the anti-Chinese movement often breaks out in Southeast Asia where Chinese entrepreneurs have delivered outstanding performance. After Southeast Asian countries regained their political independence from colonists after WWII, the new governments have economically restrained Chinese entrepreneurs in many aspects in order to protect the interests of the natives. For instance, only native people are allowed to engage in certain industries. The restraints will not be canceled in the short term. Secondly, along with advancements in education in these places, natives are more and more educated, so Chinese entrepreneurs show decreasing advantages in human and social capitals. In addition, economic globalization ultimately blurs national boundaries and incites fiercer international competition.

At the same time, Chinese entrepreneurs are embracing newer opportunities in the 21st century, which are closely related to the rejuvenation of China.

Firstly, it is possible for China to maintain an economic growth at a rate between 8% and 10% for another two or three decades, and become the world's largest economy by 2030 if China continues to maintain political stability and adheres to reform and opening up, despite hurdles. If this vision can be realized, China's economic development will bring many opportunities to overseas Chinese entrepreneurs. Although China has entered the World Trade Organization (WTO) and has agreed to provide equitable national treatment to all the foreign entrepreneurs in investment and operation, the treatment only exists in laws. Their operations in China largely depends on the understanding of the local culture and society and proper communication with local people, so overseas Chinese entrepreneurs have a major advantage in these aspects. A key characteristic of the Confucian culture is the propagation of the continuity of its culture by future generation of families. Thus, although these overseas Chinese entrepreneurs have lived in foreign countries for a long time, they have been educated in the Confucian culture. Most communities of overseas Chinese entrepreneurs are predominant in Southeast Asia and some other areas. They share the same cultural background with domestic Chinese entrepreneurs. This is why a comparatively large proportion of the direct foreign investment comes from overseas Chinese entrepreneurs, especially in the early stages of reform and opening up. However, Europeans and Americans do not know how to communicate in China since the "laws" of China are different from their own. In the early 1990s, the author participated in various meetings abroad that were attended by leaders of the Top 500 enterprises listed in *Wealth*.

Some of the leaders were of the view that they could rely on their shares in the Chinese market to remain in the Top 500 enterprises one or two decades later, if China would continue to grow at such a rapid rate. At the same time, these leaders hesitated about their investments in China owing to the imperfect legal system. The Chinese pay particular attention to the "affection, reason, and laws", where laws are less important than the former two. Overseas Chinese entrepreneurs are used to this cultural tradition, so they were able to invest in China earlier than other foreign entrepreneurs. They regard China as their export base, owing to its rich and cheap labor and the domestic market.

Although the legal system of China has improved after China's entry into the WTO, qualified personnel are required to explain and implement laws. Foreigners can hardly handle the human relations in businesses, whereas overseas Chinese entrepreneurs are well trained in this. The rejuvenation of China would bring opportunities for the development of enterprises all around the world, but would mostly benefit overseas Chinese entrepreneurs because of their common cultural tradition and common communication experiences with China. Economic exchange is essentially the exchange of information and trust and the exchange between people based on culture. The common cultural background urges overseas Chinese entrepreneurs to show more concern to their motherland's economic development and share opportunities brought about by its economic development. Secondly, many advantages exist for Chinese entrepreneurs in the Southeast Asian countries, where many Chinese entrepreneurs are located. The main potential for the rapid growth rate of 8% to 10% of China's Gross Domestic Product (GDP) comes from the late-development advantage in terms of technological innovation. China can introduce some technologies from foreign countries as the capital accumulates and upgrade its industries and technologies, thus improving the comparative advantage. The income level of Southeast Asian countries is a little higher than China, so China can transfer their technologies to China for industrial upgrading and create a larger development space. Take Hong Kong for example, where 6 million people currently live. Hong Kong was once a labor-intensive manufacturing center, but it has transferred almost all of its manufacturing industry to the mainland after reform and opening up. Therefore, the personnel engaged in manufacturing only account for less than 10% of Hong Kong labor, but more than 20 million workers have been employed in the Pearl River Delta by Hong Kong entrepreneurs. It is the same with Taiwan entrepreneurs running businesses in the mainland. Taiwan was previously the world manufacturing center of sports shoes, but now its shoemaking industry has been mostly transferred to the mainland. Only a few large factories employ 10,000 workers in Taiwan, compared to quite a few shoe factories currently hiring more than 100,000 workers on the mainland.

In addition to technologies, the market is another important determinant for the economic development of China, including overseas and domestic markets. Regarding the overseas market, the overseas Chinese market excels at selling Chinese products overseas, because the overseas Chinese entrepreneurs know about such markets very well; the overseas market is their local market! For the domestic market, along with the increasing income level of the Chinese, the scale is expanding and there are stringent quality requirements. Since overseas Chinese entrepreneurs enjoy a little higher income than their China-based counterparts, they can introduce some mature products to the mainland, where people require high-quality products based on their increasing incomes. The brand of Chef Kang Instant Noodles is a classic example.

Among the Top 500 enterprises of the world in 2002, America was ranked 192, i.e., 38.4% of the total number, compared to America's economic share of 31.4% of the global economic aggregate. Japan was ranked 88, i.e., 17.6% of the total number, compared to its economic share of 14.5% of the global economic aggregate, which showed the connection between the two proportions. If China can catch up with America in the economic aggregate by 2030, it is possible that 100 Chinese enterprises could rank among the Top 500 enterprises of the world, which may include 70 or 80 domestic enterprises and 20 or 30 overseas Chinese enterprises that are closely related to the mainland. Currently, most overseas Chinese entrepreneurs are located in countries of small economic scale, so they mainly run businesses in the form of medium- or small-sized enterprises. The rise of the Chinese economy in the 21st century is a major opportunity for the development of overseas Chinese entrepreneurs.

Chapter 4

Curb Overheating to Prevent Supercooling*

According to the goal of the macroeconomic management of high growth and low inflation found in economics textbooks, China's economic situation was prosperous in 2003, when its Gross Domestic Product (GDP) reached 9.1% — the highest in the world. In the same year, the retail price index of commodities dropped by 0.1%, whereas the consumer price increased by only 1.2%. Profits from enterprises, fiscal incomes, and foreign trade grew significantly. In the first quarter of 2004, the GDP had grown at a rate of 9.8% compared to the same period in the previous year, while the retail price index and the consumer price index only rose by 1.4% and 2.8%, respectively.

However, economists hold different views on the current macroeconomic situation. Some consider that the government should adopt powerful measures to inhibit economic overheating, which has already emerged while some others believe that China has finally escaped deflation, which it had experienced since 1998, and has begun a new round of rapid growth. So it is necessary to protect the enthusiasm of enterprises and local governments to continue to support rapid economic growth.

The factors contributing to the rapid growth and low inflation since 2003 and the possible results should be taken into consideration to judge which of the above statements are true.

China had experienced deflation and weak non-governmental investment and consumption since the end of 1997. The national economy had maintained an average growth rate of 7.8% for five years based on the active

---

* This chapter was originally published in the *Newsletter of the China Center for Economic Research of Beijing University*, 13th issue of 2004 (429th issue of history).

financial policies duly employed by the government, which had stimulated the demands on investment. The rapid growth in 2003 was completely spurred by investments, when the investment on fixed assets had increased from 11.8% in 2002 to 26.7%, reaching the maximum growth rate of the real investment since reform and opening up. According to the expenditure approach, capital formed 39.4% of GDP in 2002, so the economic growth that was spurred by investment in 2003 had reached 10%.

The growth of investment in 2003 was mainly concentrated in three fields: real estate sector, with an investment growth rate of 29.7%; automobile sector, 87.2%; and building materials with 96.5% growth in steel materials, 92.5% in electrolytic aluminum, and 121.9% in cement. The growth of investment on building materials was stimulated by the investment growth in real estate and automobile sector. The following causes have contributed to the rapid growth of investment in real estate and automobile projects. Firstly, after the change in the government during the 16th National Congress of the Communist Party of China (CPC), the new leaders initiated municipal works. The most important factor was the investment impulse of private enterprises, which was spurred by two aspects. In 2003, sales in real estate had increased by 34.1% and the sales in the automobile sector had increased by 68.5%. In addition, the four major state-owned banks decided to go public and increased their loans to lower the proportion of bad debts. As a result of this, many projects with investments worth several billions or tens of billions of yuan were launched in real estate, automobile sector, and building materials.

The hot sale in real estate and automobile sector in 2003 was related to the opening up of consumer credit. The consumption hot spot has changed several times since reform and opening up. Based on the income levels of urban residents, they should have invested in real estate and automobiles in the late 1990s. In foreign countries, employees buy houses and cars when they are able to afford the mortgage loan with a projected repayment with their future income. However, in China's banking system, the four major state-owned banks or the 13 subsequent joint-equity banks mainly provide loans to enterprises, especially the state-owned banks. Residents cannot obtain credit loans for real estate and automobile consumption. Therefore, after 20 years, China has accumulated a large stock of demands by a group of people who should have engaged in the consumption of commercial houses and cars, but failed because of the lack of corresponding support from the credit loans. In 2003, the banks opened their credit service on real estate and automobile consumption. This stimulated the consumption, absorbed the excessive production capacity, solved the deflation problem, and resulted in the super growth in the demand for real estate and automobiles. Similar to the discharge of water from the reservoir, it was expected that the super growth in these sectors would be followed by regular growth. However, the investment on real estate and automobile projects for 2003 and the following years was designed based on the growth rate of 30%, 40%, or even 60% and 70%. Even under the hot sale of houses and cars in 2003, there were some new products that remained unsold, thereby rendering a large amount of unmarketable houses and cars after the completion of the new round of projects. Investments in real estate and automobile projects would necessarily compress, while investments in building materials would definitely lead to over production. The proportion of banks' bad debts would significantly rebound.

The overheating of investments in real estate and automobiles in 2003 led to a significant rise in the prices of building materials and even caused production to halt thus limiting the consumption in many areas, but the excessive production capacity and oversupply since 1998 were not eliminated. Therefore, overall inflation was inhibited. It was difficult for the academic circles and various macro-management departments to reach a consensus based on favorable macro indicators, so the overly rapid growth of investment continued in the first quarter of 2004. If the overheating of investments in real estate, automobiles, and building materials is not been timely inhibited, the new production capacity upon the completion of these projects would worsen the excessive production capacity and deflation in various fields. It is extremely necessary to adopt macro-control measures.

In 2004, some economic fields overheated, while others overcooled, so it was difficult to conduct macroeconomic management to cool the overheating and vice-versa. Cuts in credit, investments, and projects adopted in the planned economy age, as well as during the early stages of reform and opening up, cannot substantially solve the problem. This is because problems will emerge once the measure is no longer adopted, and shall not be adopted in the socialist market economy, though it is effective in inhibiting overheating.

The currency policy is the key strategy for the government to manage the overheating of the macro economy in the market economy. Since the latter half of 2003, the People's Bank has raised the proportion of the deposit reserves three times and offset the monetary base released by an increase in foreign exchange reserves with the central bank's bills, in order to reduce the loanable funds of commercial banks. However, the four major state-owned commercial banks (the main force of the banking industry) have prepared excessive reserves, and the speed of the currency circulation has been facilitated under the economic overheating, so the expansion of bank loans has not been effectively inhibited by measures such as the increase of the deposit reserves. Another way is to increase the interest rate. If the interest rates for loans and deposits are increased at the same time, the demand on investment and loans cannot be controlled since most enterprises seeking loans only care whether they can obtain loans instead of the interest rate. Meanwhile, savers are sensitive to the interest rate on their deposits, so an increase in the interest rates would necessarily increase the deposits, reduce demand of consumables, and inhibit the consumption. Therefore, the measure cannot cool the overheating, but would further cool the overcooling. Another method is to raise the interest rate for loans, but retain the current interest rate for deposits, which would not influence savings or the enterprises that aim to obtain loans. The increasing gap between the deposit and loan interest rates would encourage the banks to provide more loans, which would oppose the goal to control the overgrowth of loans.

Under China's current circumstances, the main measure to inhibit the overheating of investment should be to apply window guidance and strengthen commercial banks' role in checking, approving, and supervising loans. China has already provided the provision that enterprises can apply for loans from banks only if they can invest their own funds in projects. The provision was not carried out previously, but should be implemented now.

For overcooling the economy, the most effective way to control deflation is to encourage demands from the rural areas. The biggest stock demand of China currently lies in rural consumption. The restraints include limited rural consumption, the low income of peasants, and the seriously insufficient construction of infrastructure related to consumption in rural areas, including the rich rural areas. The undergoing rural taxation reform and the exemption of the agricultural taxes will facilitate the increase of peasants' incomes. With regard to the construction of infrastructure in rural areas, the 16th National Congress of the CPC proposed the goal of building an all-around, affluent society. There are difficulties in achieving this goal in the rural areas. Therefore, the Party has focused in prioritizing works in rural areas. More long-term construction bonds will be distributed to facilitate the construction of infrastructure related to production and living in rural areas.

Finally, local governments at all levels should penetrate further in gaining a scientific understanding of development in order to achieve an overall coordinated sustainable development, rather than short-term and unsustainable performance and image. This could be done by cooperating with the window guidance provided by the banks, stopping the unfavorable items, increasing the incomes of the peasants, and enhancing rural infrastructure.

It was believed that as long as the central government and the whole nation, from the leadership to the masses, reached a consensus, China would usher in rapid growth and low inflation in 2004 and for the next several years based on the efforts in the above-mentioned aspects.

Chapter 5

Window Guidance and Macro Control* — Contemplating the Current Macroeconomic Policies of China

1. Failure to Reach Expected Effect by Raising the Interest Rate

The effect of macro control gradually reveals itself. The next step is to continue to consolidate the outcomes and finally realize the "soft landing" of the Chinese economy. The argument on whether the economy was overheating in 2003 and whether macro control should be conducted has come to an end. The fact that the investment growth rate in the first quarter of 2004 reached 43% shows that it is very necessary and timely for the government to conduct macro control. However, at the current critical moment, a new argument on which methods shall be employed in the macro control has appeared. Two different opinions exist. Some believe that the market means shall be applied, such as to lower the investment impulse by adjusting the interest rate, while others think that in a country of mature market economy, increasing the interest rate is not enough to inhibit overly rapid growth of investment. The author holds the second view regarding the current economic environment of China.

It is not enough to conduct macro control only through market means. The situation is beyond that as China has entered the market economy. The methods of the market economy shall be applied especially where most investments come from private economies. Halting investments, projects,

---

*This chapter was originally published in the *Newsletter of the China Center for Economic Research of Beijing University*, 33rd issue of 2004 (449th issue of history).

and credit adopted in the planned economy age, as well as during the early stages of reform and opening up, cannot substantially solve the problem. In order to maintain the growth of the national economy, the government has to release control over investment and credit, else the problem will emerge once the measure is no longer adopted. Then, another round of implementation of the measure shall start again. The violent ups and downs will incur great losses to the national economy. In the mature market economy, government's main measures for the macro control include the currency and financial policies. However, it is not enough to conduct macro control only by market means under China's current circumstances. In the author's opinion, the following factors are taken into consideration.

Firstly, measures, including the rise in loan provision, have failed to inhibit the expansion of the bank loans. Since the latter half of 2003, the People's Bank has raised the proportion of the deposit reserves three times and offset the monetary base released by the increase of foreign exchange reserves with the central bank's bills, in order to reduce the loanable funds of commercial banks. However, the four major state-owned commercial banks (the main force of the banking industry) have prepared excessive reserves, and the speed of the currency circulation has been facilitated under economic overheating, so the general currency supply in the first quarter of 2004 was increased by 19.1% compared to the same period in 2003, a supply that is higher than 17% of the goal confirmed at the beginning of the year. The RMB loans of financial institutions have reached 834.2 billion yuan, 23.8 billion yuan higher than the same period of the previous year. In addition, the monthly weighted average interest rate of the interbank lending market has been lowered slightly, having demonstrated the relaxed market capitals.

Secondly, increasing the interest rate cannot lower the investment. Since the measures, including the rise of the provision for loans, have failed to reach the expected effect and the interest rate is the core of the currency policy in common market economy, the majority asks to inhibit the overheating of investment by increasing the interest rate. However, based on detailed analysis, it is difficult to reach the expected result by increasing the interest rate under China's current circumstances.

There are two ways to increase the interest rate. Firstly, increase the interest rates for loans and deposits at the same time. In terms of loans, though private departments conduct the investment with enterprises as the investment subject, their capitals mostly come from bank loans. The projects in steel and electrolytic aluminum, which need large investments, will create demands by the investment, resulting in a constant growth in demand and prices, inducing the upsurge of non-government investment. They have a high expectation on the profit rate and would plan to recover the investment cost after one or two years of operation. Since investment relies on bank loans, it is impossible to inhibit investment by raising the interest rate higher than their expected return rate. Moreover, most enterprises are only interested in securing loans and do not care about the interest rate, which is a lesson learned by private enterprises. Enterprises often try many tactics to obtain loans. If they succeed in running the projects, they will return the loan, but if they fail, they will not pay off the debt. They are not sensitive to the loan interest rate, so the rise in interest rates cannot inhibit the demands on investment and loans. However, savers are very sensitive to the interest rate of deposits. The interest rate of the national debt is 0.5% higher than the interest rate of fixed deposits, so many people withdraw money and queue for the national debt. Therefore, the rise in the interest rates of deposits will lead to a significant growth in savings. The difficulty of the macroeconomic control in 2004 was to inhibit the overheating of investment in some aspects, simultaneously stimulating the consumption and controlling the oversupply of most consumer goods. The rise in interest rates cannot control the overheating, but will further cool the overcooling.

Another possible way is to increase the interest rate for loans, but retain the current interest rate for deposits, which will not influence savings and thus avoid cooling the overcooling. It also shows no influence on the enterprises that aim to obtain loans. The increasing gap between the deposit and loan interest rates will encourage the banks to provide more loans, which will oppose the goal to control the overgrowth of loans.

2. Striking Effect of Window Guidance

The author believes that the government has adopted normal methods in the current macro control. Soft budget constraints affect most Chinese economic subjects in different degrees, including local governments, state-owned enterprises, and private enterprises. The profits and risk control are not the only goals of state-owned banks. Many market-based instruments in countries of mature market economy cannot attain the expected result in China. If the interest rate of loans is uniquely determined by the supply and demand of capitals in the market, then high interest rates will be levied for projects of high risk and speculation, at the same time, loans will be provided to investment projects of low risks. Capital will flow into projects of higher risks and speculation, which is the problem of adverse selection. Even in America, Japan, and European countries of mature market economy, the interest rate of loans is not completely dependent on the supply and demand of capital. To avoid the problem of adverse selection, the interest rate of loans in banks is lower than the equilibrium interest rate of the market, so as to enable the demand on capital to exceed the supply of capital. Then, the banks will decide whether to provide loans based on various "non-market" means of inspection, including verifying the credit worthiness of the enterprises applying for loans, proportion of their own capital, market risks, and the expected return of projects. It is not practical to allocate the bank loans completely through the market mechanism or to anyone that is willing to pay higher interest rate to obtain the loans. For the monetary authorities in countries of mature market economy, they can adjust the demand on investment by the market interest rate, because they have fully given play to the banks' role in supervising the risks and returns of the projects and have well understood the economic conditions. Therefore, if they increase the interest rate, the projects of lower investment return cannot obtain loans, and on the contrary, if they lower the interest rate, more projects can obtain loans. Only under these circumstances can the currency policy can effectively control the investment scale.

The following are the advantages and disadvantages of an investment project dependent on the market demand and competition in the future, and the promises made by the borrowers for the project. The proportion of the enterprise's own funds shall be taken into consideration for the selection and approval of loans by the bank. If the enterprise's own funds account for 50% or 20% of the total investment, the enterprise will bear a great loss if the investment fails, so the investor will be very cautious in selecting the project and the bank will share fewer risks. In the financial crisis of East Asia in 1998, since the Hong Kong banking industry had strictly followed the financial supervision authority's requirements on the proportion of the enterprise's own funds and the proportion of loans on real estate projects in the total loan amount, the banking industry had not been greatly attacked, despite the crash of the real estate bubbles. By comparison, other countries and regions that did not strictly follow these requirements suffered the biggest blow.

The Chinese government has stated for a long time that enterprises could only apply for loans based on their own certain capitals. For example, 20% of self-owned capitals, approval of land, and certain degree of land leveling are required for real estate projects applying for bank loans, while 25% of self-owned capitals for steel sector and 20% of self-owned capitals for cement sector are required. However, in order to lower the proportion of bad debt, the four major state-owned commercial banks, as the core of the financial industry of China, released their requirements on self-owned capitals and the selection of projects and provided loans for some projects of high risks. Therefore, it is necessary to give play to commercial banks' role in inspecting the loan projects under the overly rapid growth rate of loans and investments in China. The proportion of self-owned capitals should be increased according to the current macroeconomic situation, in order to increase the proportion of self-owned capitals in the steel sector to 40%, cement industry to 35%, and housing industry to 35%. Meanwhile, the banks should strictly follow the policies. The window guidance will show a more obvious result than the adjustment of the interest rate. Investments in May 2004 decreased to 18.3%, compared to the 43% in the first quarter. Considering the effect of SARS (severe acute respiratory syndrome) in 2003 that lowered the investment in May 2003, the outcome of the decrease in investments in May 2004 is even more obvious.

It is a goal of China's macro control to adopt window guidance and give full play to commercial banks' role in inspecting and approving loan projects. However, it should be noted that the banks would not stop all projects, but would provide loans to enterprises with adequate self-owned funds and projects with high returns, according to the conditions of different projects, and would discontinue the provision of loans to projects of insufficient self-owned capitals and low expected returns. Therefore, China will not follow the old pattern of "cut up loans, investment, and projects", which could be ruinous.

The growth rate of investment in 2004 significantly decreased under window guidance. This means a "hard landing" for investment, but is a "soft landing" for the economic growth if banks continue to provide loans to projects meeting the requirements on self-owned capitals and expected returns. The author estimates that the consumption would grow by 7% to 8%, the investment would grow by 15% to 20%, and the GDP would continue to increase by above 9% in 2004, while the GDP growth rate in 2005 would be expected to exceed 8%. Moreover, after the current macro control, if the banks regard the profits and risk control as the operation goal and conduct necessary inspections on the credit worthiness of enterprises, proportion of the self-owned capitals, and returns and risks of the projects, and meanwhile if the budget constraints for various economic subjects can be set up, the monetary authority of China will be able to control the macro economy by adjusting the interest rates.

Chapter 6

Will the Reform of Exchange Rate Regime of RMB be Successful?*

The government began to apply the new policy on the exchange rate on July 21, 2005, which increased the exchange rate from RMB8.27 : US$1 to RMB8.11 : US$1, with a slight appreciation of 2%, meanwhile "restoring" the managed floating system and "referring to" instead of "depending on" a basket of currencies. The key to whether a reform of the exchange rate policy can reach government's expectation, i.e., whether the RMB exchange rate will no longer be a huge international political or economic issue, lies in whether China can conduct the long-term and slow adjustment of the exchange rate by a small margin (similar to that in 1994 to 1997) instead of following Japan's and Chinese Taiwan's earlier strategy of mid-1980s when they conducted rapid and constant appreciation over a short time. This depends on whether the international speculative pressure on the appreciation of RMB can be eliminated. If China can eliminate the speculative pressure and conduct a long-term and slow adjustment of the managed exchange rate according to the economic development and foreign trade in China, the reform of the exchange rate policy, this time, would be successful.

Since 1994, China has merged the exchange rates and adopted the managed floating exchange rate. The exchange rate of RMB8.7 : US$1 in 1994 was increased to around 8.29 in 1997, a 5% rise in four years. Will the current reform of the exchange rate policy continue with the mode of fine-tuning the exchange rate according to the actual economic variations, such as the trade, prices, and comparison of productivity?

---

*This chapter was summarized based on the presentations made in the quarterly meeting of "China's Economic Observation" held at the China Center for Economic Research of Beijing University on July 30, 2005.

To answer this question, the question of why RMB has become the international focus in recent years, will be explained first. The problem of the RMB exchange rate includes two levels: the exchange rate management system and the exchange rate level. According to the theory on international finance and empirical studies, the most favorable exchange rate system for developing countries is the managed floating exchange rate system, which was adopted by China during the merging of exchange rates in 1994. When the financial crisis in East Asia broke out in 1997, the currencies in most Asian countries and regions devaluated, and the international monetary speculation organizations estimated that the RMB would also be devaluated. However, China resolutely promised not to devaluate the RMB and therefore the exchange rate of RMB was fixed at the lower limit of the managed floating system. After 2002, the international speculative forces estimated the appreciation of RMB, but the Chinese government did not bend to the pressure and fixed the exchange rate of RMB at the upper limit of the managed floating system. When the speculative pressure disappears, the exchange rate of RMB would be naturally restored to the original managed floating rate and adjusted according to the economic conditions in China.

The international speculation over the devaluation of the RMB after 1997 was derived from the estimation of the "domino effect" of the financial crisis in East Asia. The current speculation over appreciation is derived from both political and commercial aspects. Politically, the Japanese government was the first to propose the undervaluation of RMB, leading to an output deflation of China during the "Finance Ministers' Meeting of Seven Countries" in March 2003, which set off a wave of pressure on the appreciation of RMB. Actually, China's export only accounts for less than 5% of the world and cannot be regarded as the origin of international deflation, even if the goods were sold at rock bottom prices. The American government exerted pressure on China and stated that the undervaluation of RMB incurred huge trade deficit and increased the unemployment rate of America. In fact, the appreciation of RMB would not solve the trade deficit or increase the employment rate of America, because China and America produce different products and China mainly sells labor-intensive products to America, which are not currently produced by America. The commercial speculative pressure on appreciation of RMB is also found economically groundless. The trade surplus of China in recent years was US$12.2 billion in 1996, US$40.4 billion in 1997, US$43.5 billion in 1998, US$29.2 billion in 1999, US$24.2 billion in 2000, US$22.6 billion in 2001, US$30.5 billion in 2002, US$25.5 billion in 2003, and US$31.9 billion in 2004, respectively. It can be seen that the international speculation over the devaluation of RMB occurred at the moment of large trade surplus, while the speculation over the appreciation occurred at the time of small trade surplus. If it was indeed the RMB deviating from the equilibrium exchange rate that contributed to the international speculation over RMB, it should be the speculation over the appreciation of RMB in 1997 and 1998 and over the devaluation in 2003 and 2004. This demonstrates that the speculation over the devaluation or appreciation of RMB is not related to the deviation of RMB from the equilibrium exchange rate. It will be more evident from the perspective of the proportion of the trade surplus in gross domestic product (GDP) or the total trade volume. The author does not dare to confirm that the current RMB exchange rate is exactly the equilibrium exchange rate, but can tell that the current exchange rate is not far from the equilibrium exchange rate based on the small proportion of trade surplus in GDP.

Then, why did the international financial circles speculate on the appreciation of RMB? The apparent cause was the hot money in the international market, which flew to the East Asia before the financial crisis in China, leading to the bubbles of stock market and real estate, flew back to America and incurred the bubble of Internet after the financial crisis in the East Asia, and sought for a new way-out after the bubble of Internet broke. China has become an attractive target based on its sound economic development in recent years. More importantly, as demonstrated by previous experiences, once if America exerts pressure on any country, the exchange rate of the country would be significantly appreciated in the short term making the international financial speculators regard it as a rare opportunity, such as Japan did in 1985 after the Square Agreement.

If the current exchange rate has been undervalued by 20% to 30%, the significant value appreciation would be favorable to the Chinese economy. However, the studies show that the current exchange rate is undervalued by 2% to 3% at most, no higher than 5%. Under this condition, it is definitely unfavorable to Chinese economy, as well as the American economy, to increase the value by 15% to 20%. This is because China's economic situation is different from Japan's in the 1980s, when the development level of Japan was close to America, and their products competed with each other at the same level. The appreciation of the Japanese yen weakened the competitiveness of Japanese products in the competition with American products, which benefited America's industrial development and reduced its trade deficit. However, the current economic structure of China complements America's economic structure; China's per-capita income is US$1,300, compared to US$36,000 of America, while China mainly produces labor-intensive products, which are not produced by America. America transferred many of its imports from East Asian countries and regions to China, which contributes to China's trade surplus with America. Chinese products have not taken up the shares of American products. After the appreciation of RMB, the U.S. would have to import from China with a higher price or import from other countries, whose product prices would be necessarily higher than the current prices in China. Therefore, the appreciation of RMB would not solve the problem of unemployment, but would increase the trade deficit of America.

Some believe that both America and Japan exert pressure on China only for the sake of domestic election, in order to regard China as the scapegoat for the sluggish economy after the burst of economic bubbles. Before the reform of China's exchange rate on July 21, 2005, the American government already understood that the appreciation of RMB could not solve the trade deficit and high employment rate in America, as demonstrated by the statements made by American Treasury Secretary, John Snow and Federal Reserve Board Chairman, Alan Greenspan. In addition, after the appreciation of RMB on July 21, America announced the devaluation of U.S. dollars against the major currencies of the world and the increase of the interest rate of the 10-year national debts, which indicated that international financial speculators believed the appreciation of RMB was unfavorable to the American economy. They did not speculate on the appreciation of RMB based on the actual economic conditions.

With the practical actions over the past two years, the Chinese government has proven that China will not bow to foreign political or speculative pressure or adjust the exchange rate system that is unfavorable to China's economic development with the practical actions. American decision-makers have already realized that the appreciation of RMB could not solve the trade deficit or high unemployment rate in America, while the facts have shown that the appreciation of RMB is unfavorable to the American economy. Therefore, the American government should not exert pressure on the appreciation of RMB that would harm America. Owing to absence of a basic foundation for the speculation over RMB, there would be no estimation on the significant appreciation of RMB in the short term in the international market. At the same time, since China's capital account has not yet been opened, the speculation on RMB has to be conducted in a subtle way through an agent, so the service fee (about 5% of total amount) would be charged every year. In addition, as speculators have to give up stable profits without risks, such as the national debts of America, another 5% of the total amount is lost every year. Therefore, the cost on the speculation over the exchange rate of RMB is about 10%. Under the managed floating exchange rate system, the maximum rise of RMB value may reach 2%, based on normal conditions of economic development. Speculation on RMB would lose money as long as the RMB would not be appreciated significantly, so speculators would naturally abandon the choice. As the pressure on speculation on RMB disappears, China can restore the managed floating exchange rate system that started since 1994 and adjust the value of RMB by a small margin based on trade and economic conditions, such as the adoption of a basket of currencies.

Chapter 7

Commercial Environment Construction and Macroeconomic Development*

China has embraced rapid development of foreign-oriented business since the reform and opening up. Foreign trade has seen an annual growth rate of 16.7% from 1978 to 2004. The total volume of foreign trade has grown 56 times, from US$20.6 billion in 1978 to US$1.61548 trillion in 2004. China was ranked only the 35th of the world trade in 1978, but it jumped to the third place in 2004. Evidently, great changes have occurred in these years.

The internal trade has also developed rapidly. In 1952, the total retail sales of China amounted to RMB26.2 billion yuan, which grew to 158.8 billion yuan by 1978, and 1.0993 trillion yuan by 1992. Since then, the retail sales in China have stepped into a stage of rapid growth, which increased to 2.062 trillion yuan in 1995, 3.1113 trillion in 1999, 4.2027 trillion in 2002, and 5.395 trillion in 2004. The famous "Moore's Law" in information industry states that the speed and memory capacity of chips will double every 18 months. There seems to exist a similar law in China's business development. The total retail sales of China reached 1.545 trillion yuan in the 6th Five-Year Plan between 1981 and 1986, 3.461 trillion yuan during the 7th Five-Year Plan, 6.9756 trillion in the 8th Five-Year Plan, and 14.6513 trillion yuan in the 9th Five-Year Plan. The figure has doubled every five years.

---

*This chapter was summarized with the help of Shi Tuo, based on the presentations made in the 2nd Business Development Forum of China held in Beijing on November 19, 2005 and originally published in the *Newsletter of the China Center for Economic Research of Beijing University*, 77th issue of 2005 (526th issue).

The primary cause for the growth in internal trade lies in the rapid rise of national incomes. The gross domestic product (GDP) has increased 10.3 times in the 26 years after reform and opening up, with an annual growth rate of 9.4%, while the domestic per-capita incomes have reached an annual growth rate of 8%. Therefore, the demands increase thereupon.

The second cause is the extreme improvement of the business environment. In terms of the hardware environment, key infrastructure, such as traffic, transportation, and information, have developed rapidly. In 1978, the total domestic mileage of railways amounted only to 51,700 km, which has grown by 40% (to 74,400 km) in 2004. During the same period, the total mileage of highways has increased from 890,000 km to 1.87 million km, including the extremely rapid development of the expressway, from 0 km in 1988 to 34,300 km in 2004, ranking the second of the world, only after America. Civil aviation has also developed swiftly. The mileage of civil aviation has grown from 149,000 km in 1978, when domestic flights were rare and foreign flights were so inconvenient that passengers had to transfer in London or Paris to go to America, to 2.05 million km in 2004, enough to span the equator 50 times. The communication and information industry has also made phenomenal progress. The landline connections were also increased from 4.05 million in 1978 to 421.02 million in 2004. Mobile phones have increased from 18,000 in 1990 to 334.82 million in 2004. The Internet that started to be applied only in the mid-1990s has currently covered all provinces, including Tibet, and even all counties in provinces on the southeast coast of China.

In terms of policies, the improving position of private economy has demonstrated the progress in software development. At the beginning of reform and opening up, the private economy had only become a complement upon fierce discussions. The private economy only obtained the same "unshaken" status as the state-owned economy by the 16th National Congress of Communist Party of China, when it was confirmed to unswervingly develop state-owned economy and meanwhile unswervingly guide and develop private economy.

The constant improvements in hardware and software have played a decisive guiding role in the rapid growth of trade and business. However, the differences between the growth of internal and external trade have called for deep deliberations. Firstly, the growth of external trade is much faster than the growth of internal trade and the growth of the national economy. In the recent two decades, the annual growth rate of external trade has reached 16.7%, compared to the annual growth rate of GDP of 9.4%. Secondly, the growth of internal trade is slower than the growth of the national economy. Based on the current price, the total domestic retail sales have increased from 155.8 billion yuan in 1978 to 5.395 trillion yuan in 2004. If calculated with the fixed price, the total domestic retail sales actually only amounted to more than 1 trillion yuan in 2004, which is 7.1 times higher than that of 1978, compared to the growth of GDP of 10.3 times within the same period. The annual growth rate of domestic retail sales has reached 7.8%, 1.6% lower than the annual growth rate of GDP, which is 9.4%. The two characteristics and relevant statistics have clearly illustrated why the consumption currently accounts only for 53% of GDP, 18% lower than the world average level.

What, then, is the problem? The problem mainly lies in the unsatisfying business environment of China, especially the business environment for internal trade. The World Bank and the international financial companies began to conduct a worldwide survey on the global business environment in 2002. The results released by the World Bank in early 2005 showed that China was ranked 91st among the 155 countries and regions of the survey, with New Zealand, Singapore, and the U.S. occupying the first three places.

The current level of China cannot be compared to the developed countries that currently hold the first places, but some points can be figured out based on a careful analysis over the whole ranking. For example, among the developing countries that belong to the East Asian economic circle, as China does, Thailand was ranked 20th and Malaysia was ranked 21st; among the transforming countries that are in the same development stage with China, Lithuania was ranked 15th, Latvia was ranked 26th, Slovakia was ranked 37th, Czech Republic was ranked 41st, and Poland was ranked 54th; and as a part of China, Hong Kong was ranked 7th, while Taiwan was ranked 35th. In the above perspectives, the business environment of the inland of China is comparatively low, which should be further improved.

In the evaluation, China's ranking in 10 specific indicators also provoked further thinking. China was ranked 126th in the complexity to commence a business, the latter in the rank list the more complicated; ranked 136th in the complexity to obtain the license for the construction; ranked 87th in the employment of workers; ranked 24th in the amount of registered capitals; ranked 113th in the complexity of financing; ranked 100th in the protection of investors; ranked 119th in the taxation; ranked 48th in the cross-border trade; ranked 47th in the implementation of contracts; and ranked 59th in the complexity to close the enterprises. The above statistics show that the indicators for the software environment of business have lowered China's ranks, as they are generally below the average rank of the list. Any indicator behind the 91st rank constitutes the main obstruction for China's development of internal trade.

According to the investigation in 2004, China requires 13 seals (or clearances) from 13 departments to start an enterprise, compared to 6.5 seals in the developed countries. It would also take 48 days to go through formalities to start an enterprise, compared to 19.5 days in the developed countries. How much would it cost to run through the formalities to start an enterprise in China? It costs 13.6% of the annual per-capita income in China, compared to 6.8% of the developed countries. The bank deposits to start an enterprise in China require 9.47 times that of the per-capita income of US$1,277, compared to 41.2% of the per-capita income in developed countries. China requires 30 seals, 146 days, and a cost of 126% of the annual per-capita income to obtain a license for construction, compared to 4.1 seals, 146 days, and 75.1% in developed countries. Chinese enterprises should submit 46.9% of gross profits as taxes, only a little higher than the developed countries that submit 45.4%. However, there are too many tax items and highly complicated formalities in China. Chinese enterprises have to pay 34 different taxes, while developed countries only need to submit 16.9 different taxes; in addition, Chinese enterprises have to spend 584 h on matters related to taxes, while developed countries spend only 197 h for taxing. Based on the above comparison, it is evident that some aspects of the business environment could and should be improved.

It is of great strategic and practical importance to improve the business environment in China to augment the country's future development. Strategically, though China has stepped over the minimum limit of middle-income countries after the 26-year development since reform and opening up, it is still far behind the developed countries. In 2004, China's per-capita income was only US$1,277, only accounting for 3.2% of Americans' per-capita income of US$40,100. Facilitating the economic development can only gradually narrow the gap. In *Wealth of Nations*, Adam Smith had detailed on how to facilitate economic development and put the labor division in the foreground. The finer the labor division, the higher the efficiency is. When the labor division is finer, each laborer concentrates only on his own work and is more skilled in his work, and it may be more possible for the machines, equipment, and technologies to be improved. Adam Smith also stated that the level of labor division determined the market scale of a country. The bigger the market, the finer would be the labor division and efficiency.

However, the size of the market depends on the business environment, because the business environment decides the transaction cost. The expansion of the market would improve the labor division, but would meanwhile require more transactions. In an unfavorable software and hardware environment, the high transaction cost may offset the raised efficiency, which would lead to the decline of profits and inhibit the expansion of market scale. Therefore, strategically, the business environment plays a very important role in balancing the relation between the market scale and labor division.

It is also of strong practical importance to improve the business environment in the next several years. According to the author's observation and analysis, China may meet a stressful economic environment in the next one or two years. Deflation emerged in China since 1998. By 2003 and 2004, the indicators show a favorable situation for macro economy, with a GDP growth rate of 9.5%. Regarding the price index, China has recovered from deflation and avoided inflation and realized the safe "soft landing" of economy. However, the price index refers to the average ups and downs of a dozen of commodities, so a careful study is needed. Among the 16 types of commodities within the statistics for consumer prices, 4 have risen and 12 have fallen in 2003, while 6 have risen and 10 have fallen in 2004. This means that the prices of some commodities are rising sharply, while the prices of other commodities are declining owing to excessive production capacity. Although the price index seems stable, it hides risks. Investment has pulled China out of deflation in 2003 and 2004, which mainly concentrates on real estate, automobile, and building materials. The overheating investment acts as the demand before the completion of projects, but becomes the supply after the completion of projects, bringing about surplus in supply. Therefore, deflation would be inevitable, in addition to the excessive production capacity. Based on the strict definition, China has already met the deflation in September 2005, when the consumer price index was 0.9%, lower than 1%, and the commodity price index was zero. Theoretically, deflation emerges when the consumer price index is lower than one and when the commodity price index approaches zero. In 2006, it would probably prolong the situation.

Under deflation, the constantly declining commodity prices and the enterprises running under their production capacity would incur the decrease of profits, or even bankruptcy, and increase the unemployment and bad debts of banks. Therefore, enterprises should improve themselves, lower their operation cost, and improve their business environment, so as to raise the survival rate of enterprises. In addition, the Chinese government should also vigorously improve the business environment and lower the transaction cost of enterprise operation. The author proposes four suggestions here.

Firstly, the government should strictly implement the Administrative Licensing Law. It should not approve proposals that are not worthy of implementation and should strictly execute the recording system. China should learn from developed countries and try to reduce the required seals and time for enterprises.

Secondly, improve the taxation environment. China's tax rate is almost the same with developed countries, but China requires more taxation items and formalities. The government could consider enabling the enterprises contributing to internal and external trade to share the same treatment, meanwhile, transform the production-oriented value added tax to consumption-oriented value added tax.

Thirdly, vigorously develop the service industry. Although the business environment is necessary for the development of the service industry, the development of service industry itself can directly improve the business environment. The service industry includes production-, circulation-, and consumption-oriented enterprises. The consumption-oriented service industry aims to improve the quality of life of people , while the production- and circulation-oriented service industries aim to reduce the transaction cost and directly improve the business environment.

Fourthly, improve the financing environment. Currently, 23 to 24 trillion yuan are provided each year as loans, but the problem lies in that most medium- and small-sized enterprises can hardly obtain loans, owing to China's imperfect financial structure. Medium- and small-sized enterprises account for more than 10 million enterprises in China, but they can hardly obtain financing from the stock market and state-owned enterprises. Therefore, firstly, China must develop the regional private small- and medium-sized banks; secondly, develop the private guarantee industry that would solve the loan and provide security to the small- and medium-sized enterprises; thirdly, learn from developed countries, such as America or Chinese Taiwan, that the government sets up the small- and medium-sized enterprises development board to check and approve the investment plan or start-up plan for small- and medium-sized enterprises and provide financing guarantee for qualified enterprises; and fourthly, the most difficult and important, strengthen and facilitate the construction of social credit system, private enterprises, and credit assessment mechanism.

The realization of the above points would significantly improve the business environment of China and play a positive and promoting role in the country's future economic development.

Competitive Advantage, Comparative Advantage, and Economic Development Strategies*

After Michael Porter published his book *The Competitive Advantage of Nations*, the theory of competitive advantage began to exert a great impact on researchers and policy-makers worldwide. However, the followers of the theory often completely separate the comparative advantages and competitive advantages, which is incorrect and harmful to the selection of the mode of economic development by a country or a region. If a country or a region chooses a development strategy that violates its own comparative advantage, then it may prejudice its industrial competitiveness and its overall economic competitiveness.

In order to clarify the misunderstanding, the authors conducted an in-depth discussion on the relationship between the comparative advantages and competitive advantages and further revealed the role of this relationship in the selection of the road for economic development in developing countries. The authors believed that a country or a region can only create and maintain its industrial competitive advantages by giving full play to its comparative advantages.

1. Main Ideas of the Theory of Competitive Advantage

Before *The Competitive Advantage of Nations*, Michael Porter mainly focused on the study of enterprise strategies and competitiveness. He

*This chapter was the No C2003002 draft for discussion at the China Center for Economic Research of Beijing University, March 25, 2003, jointly completed with Li Yongjun.

expanded the results of his research in enterprise competitiveness to include entire industries and nations and thus formed the theory of the competitive advantage of nations.

According to Michael Porter, an enterprise should establish its competitive advantages at two different levels. The competitive advantage at a low level refers to the "competitive advantage of low cost", while the competitive advantage at a high level refers to the "competitive advantage in product differences". The competitive advantage of low cost is generally derived from the special resource advantages (low cost of labor and raw materials), production technologies, and methods that can also be used by other competitors at low costs and the development of scale economy. The competitive advantage of product differences is established by creating products that are differentiated more in accordance with the clients' requirements through constant investment and innovation on equipment, technologies, management, and marketing. He also believes that the competitive advantage of product differences, which represents a higher productivity, can bring more profits to enterprises, and can be maintained for longer time since it is difficult to be imitated, compared to the competitive advantage of low cost.

The only choice for enterprises to create competitive advantages at a high level is to continuously invest and innovate. Therefore, the environment that would be favorable to continuous investment and innovation is to create competitive advantages at a high level. In order to describe such an environment, Michael Porter proposed the model of the "diamond system" in his theory of the competitive advantage of nations.

To be specific, the "diamond system" includes four major factors. The first is the production factors, including the primary production factors (general labor and natural resources) and created production factors (knowledge resources, capital resources, and infrastructure); the second is the demand, including the structure of domestic demands, size, and growth rate of the market, demanding quality and the internationalization degree of the demand; the third is the performance of relevant industries and supporting industries, including the longitudinal support (the upstream industry's support in equipment and components for enterprises) and transverse support (similar to the enterprises' support in production cooperation and information sharing); and the fourth is the enterprise strategy, enterprise structure, and competitors, including the management philosophy, management goal, work motivation of staff, and conditions of competitors in the same industry.

Based on the "diamond system", Michael Porter explained how the enterprises or industries of a nation could obtain enduring international competitiveness. Later, Michael Porter developed his theory of enterprise competitiveness into a theory of economic development. According to his logic, the goal of the national economic development is to ensure that the income level of the people is high, which depends on the productivity of the enterprises or industries of the country. The competitive advantage at a high level enables the enterprises to attain high productivity. Hence, the national income level also relies on whether the enterprises of the country can obtain the competitive advantage at a high level.

2. Comparative Advantage is the Basis for Competitive Advantage

According to the relationship between the comparative advantage and competitive advantage as analyzed by Michael Porter's "diamond system", the author believes that the basis for a country to create and maintain the industrial competitive advantage lies in giving full play to the comparative advantage of the economy.

Firstly, in terms of the production factors, both the theories, i.e., the theory of comparative advantage and the theory of competitive advantage, attach importance to the role of the production factor in the creation of enterprises' and industries' competitiveness. The difference between the two theories lies in that the theory of competitive advantage emphasizes more on the importance of "advanced" production factors, such as the advanced human capital, i.e., the universities and research institutions. Michael Porter pointed out correctly that the advanced production factors refer to the production factors created by constant investments by the governments, enterprises, and individuals. However, to create the advanced production factors, large investment is required. The large investment can come only from the economic surplus that has been created by previous production activities of the enterprises and the whole economy. Enterprises and the economy can create maximum economic surplus by organizing production activities according to the comparative advantages of the economy. On the contrary, if the economic comparative advantage is violated, then the economic capacity to accumulate economic surplus would be damaged, thus leading to a reduction of investment on the advanced production factors. In addition, the human capital is relatively complemented with material capitals, so the advanced human capital cannot play a role without the support of material capital. As a result of this, high-cost labor would migrate to countries that have high material capital. Conversely, the new machine and equipment cannot play a role solely based on the investment on material capital without the corresponding human capital. Therefore, it is a necessary condition for the accumulation of advanced production factors to follow the comparative advantages.

Secondly, in terms of the horizontal competition, Michael Porter believed that it would pressurize enterprises to increase the investment on the advanced production factors and research and development (R&D) activities, which would facilitate the innovation of enterprises. However, a positive horizontal market competition can only be realized when the industry is accorded the economic comparative advantage. When the government decides to promote the industry to catch up and surpass others against its economic comparative advantage, it is impossible to realize the positive market competition because of the following two causes. Firstly, the surpassing enterprises can hardly obtain advantages in technologies in the short term. Secondly, these enterprises cannot establish their advantages in costs by utilizing their economic comparative advantages. As the two kinds of advantages do not exist, the enterprises in this industry cannot survive on their own in the competitive market, but rely on the protective measures of the government. The fierce competition as proposed by Michael Porter would never emerge owing to the protective measures. On the contrary, economic development in developing countries has demonstrated that the "catching-up and surpassing" industry would necessarily result in the trade monopoly. Obviously, monopoly is an easier way for the enterprises to earn profits, compared to the enhanced competitiveness and improved operational performance by innovation. Therefore, under the monopoly, enterprises of the trade are interested in protecting the monopoly by rent seeking, instead of innovation. The biggest pressure on the market competition within the trade would only appear when the country develops its economy according to its comparative advantage.

Thirdly, in terms of demand, Michael Porter listed the "experienced and critical client" as the most important content of this condition. Michael Porter believed that these clients would promote the constant innovation of enterprises. However, he did not explain why clients in some countries might be "experienced and critical", while clients in other countries might not. Actually, he regarded the factor as a completely exogenous condition, but this thought can be denied by the experiences of developing countries. The client can hardly be critical about the products from the "catching-up and surpassing" industry, where the governmental protection is often applied. Under the protective policies, the policies of the government would more or less tend to protect the companies instead of clients, which increases the cost for clients to "be critical" on products. On the other hand, the "catching-up and surpassing" is often related to monopoly. Clients have fewer choices under the monopoly. Owing to the above two points, clients can hardly be "experienced and critical".

Fourthly, the theory of the competitive advantage focuses on the significant role of the relevant and supporting industry (or industry cluster) in enterprises and industries creating the competitive advantages. It should be pointed out that an industry cluster with favorable prospects would hardly survive upon the violation against the economic development strategy of the comparative advantage. On one hand, if an industry does not meet the economic comparative advantage, it is difficult for the non-government investment to constantly make profits. If the government chooses an industry that violates its own comparative advantage or chooses production technologies that violate the economic comparative advantages of an industry, it needs to utilize the financial capital to directly establish state-owned enterprises or provide enough subsidies to private capital, which would attract them to this industry. Since the government can only establish a limited number of enterprises or provide subsidies to a limited number of enterprises, the support from relevant and supporting enterprises is not enough for catching-up and surpassing enterprises. On the other hand, the direct engagement or support of the government would necessarily lead to the problem of planning and coordination among relevant enterprises. Owing to the information asymmetry, the cost of planning and coordination may be very high, so the government may tend to assign the main production process to one or several enterprises. This is the direct cause why the catching-up and surpassing enterprises in traditional planning economy were often "large and comprehensive" or "small and comprehensive". Under these circumstances, the relevant and supporting industry or the industry cluster can hardly survive. On the contrary, more enterprises may invest in industries that are accorded the economic comparative advantages owing to the higher possibility of earning profits, so the labor division may be finer and new, relevant, or supporting enterprises would constantly emerge. Then the industry cluster may appear naturally. Therefore, the current industry clusters in Jiangsu, Zhejiang, and Guangdong, etc., actually belong to the labor-intensive industry clusters.

3. The Core of the Development Strategy is to Increase the Capital Accumulation

The theory of competitive advantage states that countries of a higher per-capita income level mostly hold the competitive advantage at a high level in certain industries. Therefore, the ultimate goal for national economic development is to establish the country's enterprises and industries with high-level competitive advantages. However, the theory of the competitive advantage does not provide the answer to the question of whether the countries or regions of low income level should go over the low-level competitive advantage and directly establish the high-level competitive advantage, or form its own high-level competitive advantage through accumulations and investments in industries where the country holds the comparative advantage. According to the above analysis, a country or a region can only realize its competitive advantage by giving full play to its comparative advantage.

The core factor in the dynamic process of the comparative advantage is the capital accumulation. It is generally believed that two factors promote economic growth and development, including the accumulation of the production factor (mainly referring to capitals) and the technological progress. Since the technological progress is often limited by the capital accumulation, the ability to accumulate capital has become the key factor in achieving economic growth and development. Actually, the dynamic process of capital accumulation is the process of dynamic changes in factor endowment and structure, and comparative advantage. The process of the economic development in a country or a region is actually the dynamic process of the development of economic comparative advantage. The enterprises and industries can only attain maximum competitive advantage and create economic surplus when they follow their own comparative advantages, and then the country or region can accumulate capital to the maximum, enable their factor endowment and structure to approach the level of the developed countries or regions, and finally realize the competitive advantage at a high level and improve the per-capita incomes.

The above analysis can be illustrated by the following comparison: Korea's Samsung has committed itself to conduct intensive R&D activities to improve the competitiveness of its products, while the TSMC (Taiwanese Semiconductor Manufacturing Company) mainly concentrates on chip processing, and invests in the innovation of production process at the low level, instead of the R&D of new products. However, despite the large investment on R&D, Samsung's operation performance cannot be compared to TSMC that invests less in R&D. On the other hand, similar to enterprises, though Korea conducts more intensive R&D activities than the Chinese Taiwan, its overall performance of economic development is no better than the Chinese Taiwan.

The above instances accord to the conclusion of this chapter. It is important to maximize the possibility of creating economic surplus and conducting capital accumulation, instead of prematurely conducting large-scale R&D in order to create the advantage in product differences. The method to maximize the ability to create economic surplus is to give full play to the comparative advantage. In view of this, the theory of competitive advantage proposes the principle of the size of domestic market and industry cluster, which is a useful reference for enterprises and countries to select their industry.

Chapter 9

Chinese State-Owned Enterprises and the Reform of Financial Institutions*

The economic reform of China lasted for more than 20 years, since the late 1970s, when the Chinese economy experienced a miraculously rapid economic growth. From 1979 to 2002, China's actual annual growth rate of gross domestic product (GDP) reached 9.4%, while the annual growth of per-capita GDP reached 8.1%. In 2002, China's total export amounted to US$325.61 billion and total import was US$295.31 billion, compared to the export of US$9.75 billion and import of US$10.89 billion in 1978, with a growth of US$315.86 billion and US$284.42 billion, respectively, and a growth rate of 15.7% and 14.7%, respectively. There has been a significant improvement in the living standards of the people, along with the rapid economic growth. The net incomes of the residents in the rural areas increased from 133.6 yuan in 1978 to 2,713 yuan in 2002, while the disposable income of the residents in the urban areas increased from 343.4 yuan in 1978 to 7,702.8 yuan in 2002, with the annual growth rate of 7.6% and 8.1%, respectively.[1]

Although China made remarkable achievements in the reform and opening up for more than two decades, there exists many problems in the economic system, which may influence the sustainable development of the Chinese economy and inhibit a stable economic growth. In addition, many new characteristics have emerged recently in the Chinese economy such as China's efforts in opening to the world after her entry into World Trade

---

*This chapter was published in the 4th issue, 4th volume of the *Quarterly Journal of Economics* (July 2005), p. 913–936, jointly completed with Li Zhibin.

[1] Statistics come from *China Monthly Economic Indicators* and *China Statistical Yearbook*.

Organization (WTO). At the beginning of a new round of economic reform, it is very important for the government and the scholars to carefully review the reform course, analyze the causes for the current economic problems, and indicate correct directions for further economic reform.

Under a complete logical frame, China's reform of state-owned enterprises and financial system has been reviewed, described, and analyzed in detail in this chapter. The author has specifically illustrated the current status of the state-owned enterprises and the financial system, the reform course, and the existing problems in Sec. 1; he has indicated the direction for the reform of China's state-owned enterprises and financial system in Sec. 3; and has reached a brief conclusion in Sec. 4.

1. China's Reform of State-Owned Enterprises: Current Status, Course, and Problems

1.1. *The current status of China's state-owned enterprises*

China has a large scale of state-owned assets. According to the Ministry of Finance, China's total amount (net value) of state-owned assets had reached 11.82992 trillion yuan by 2002, having increased 3.4 times the amount in 1991, with an annual growth rate of 14.4%, including 7.69378 trillion yuan of operating state-owned enterprises,[2] which accounts for 65% of the total amount, and 4.13614 trillion yuan of non-operating state-owned assets, which accounts for 35% of the total amount. The scale and variation tendency of state-owned assets since 1995 are recorded in Table 9.1.

As shown in Table 9.1, the growth rate of the operating state-owned assets has seen a decline since the mid-1990s, which reflects the result of the policy of "invigorating large state-owned enterprises while relaxing control over small ones". Table 9.2 summarizes the distribution of operating state-owned assets among central and local governments in 2000. The operating state-owned assets are mainly allocated in more than 170,000

---

[2]Generally, operating state-owned assets include general industrial and commercial enterprises, finance and insurance enterprises, state-owned overseas enterprises, and various construction funds; and the non-operating state-owned assets mainly refer to the state-owned assets of administrative organizations.

Table 9.1. Variation Tendency of State-Owned Assets in Recent Years (1995–2002) (Units: Trillion Yuan).

Year	1995	1996	1997	1998	1999	2000	2001	2002
Total amount of state-owned assets	5.71	6.59	7.22	8.22	9.10	9.89	10.93	11.83
Annual growth rate (%)	—	15.4	9.6	13.8	10.6	8.7	10.6	8.2
Operating state owned assets	4.51	4.99	5.41	6.24	6.44	6.86	7.31	7.69
Annual growth rate (%)	—	10.8	8.3	15.4	3.3	6.5	6.6	5.2
Non-operating state-owned assets	1.20	1.60	1.81	1.98	2.65	3.02	3.62	4.14
Annual growth rate (%)	—	32.5	13.6	9.3	33.9	14.1	19.6	14.4

Source: Announcements of the Ministry of Finance.

Table 9.2. Scale and Distribution of the Operating State-Owned Assets in China (2000) (Unit: Yuan).

Item	Total amount of China	Central government	Proportion (%)	Local government	Proportion (%)
Total	6.86126 trillion	4.07685 trillion	59.4	2.78441 trillion	40.6
General industrial and commercial enterprises	5.75544 trillion	3.06904 trillion	53.3	2.6864 trillion	46.7
Finance and insurance enterprises	830.39 billion	746.76 billion	89.9	83.63 billion	10.1
Overseas enterprises	119.57 billion	105.19 billion	88.0	14.38 billion	12.0
Construction funds	155.86 billion	155.86 billion	100.0	—	—

Source: Zhang Zhuoyuan and Lu Yao (2003). Actively promoting the reform of state-owned enterprises. *Collected Essays on Finance and Economics*, (1).

state-owned enterprises in all localities and industries within China. A main characteristic for the distribution of state-owned assets, as revealed by Table 9.2, is that most assets of the finance and insurance institutions belong to the central government. Considering that China's financial organizations are mostly solely state owned or state holding, the central government has controlled most of its financial assets.

Despite the large scale of state-owned enterprises' assets, the status of state-owned enterprises in the national economy has been constantly declining during the more than 20 years period since the reform and opening up. In addition, the growth performance of the state-owned enterprises lags behind other enterprises.

Firstly, the proportion of the number of public-owned enterprises (including state-owned and collectively owned enterprises) is declining in all enterprises. In particular, after 1990, the number of non-public-owned enterprises showed a good momentum of accelerated growth, from 2.1% in 1991 to 54.6% in 2001. The proportion of the number of public-owned enterprises has declined from its initially dominating status at the beginning of the reform and opening up to 45.4% by 2001 (*China Industrial Economic Statistical Yearbook*, 2002).

Secondly, the growth rate of the total industrial output value of public-owned enterprises is lower than other enterprises. The growth rate of the total industrial output value of various economies from 1981 to 2001 has been summarized in Fig. 9.1, which shows that the growth rate of the total industrial output value of privately owned enterprises in the rural and urban areas and other types of enterprises is far higher than the public-owned economy, so the proportion of the total industrial output value of public-owned enterprises has been constantly declining. In 1980, the proportion of the total industrial output value of public-owned enterprises (state-owned and collectively owned) reached 99.5%, which declined to 90.2% by 1990, and to 54.9% by 2001 (*China Industrial Economic Statistical Yearbook*, 2002).

At the same time, the distribution of rural and urban labor in enterprises of different economic ownership has significantly changed. By the end of 2001, the total number of employees in urban state-owned and collectively owned enterprises had reached 89 million (in 1979, they were 100 million); while the number of employees in other types of enterprises had grown to

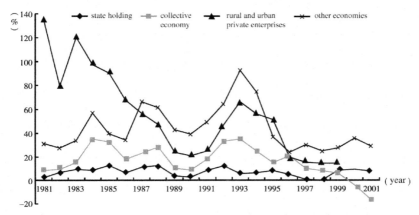

Figure 9.1. Growth Rate of the Total Industrial Output Value of Economies of Different Ownership (1981–2001).
Source: China Industrial Economic Statistical Yearbook, 2002.

58 million, accounting for 40% of the urban employment (*China Statistical Yearbook*).

Major problems among the Chinese state-owned enterprises relate to serious losses suffered by enterprises and decline of profitability. Generally, the state-owned economy makes low and declining economic profits. The profit ratio of the net fixed assets of state-owned industrial enterprises amounted to 23.2% in 1980, which had surprisingly declined to 6.0% by 2001, compared to 8.4%, the profit ratio of the net fixed assets of nationwide industrial enterprises (*China Industrial Economic Statistical Yearbook*, 2002). Considering the artificial increase of the book profits owing to the policy of "three-year difficulty relief" for state-owned enterprises, the net profit ratio of state-owned enterprises' assets has never exceeded 5% after 1994.

1.2. *Course of China's reform of state-owned enterprises*

China's reform of state-owned enterprises has lasted for more than 20 years, with the initial thrust to deal with "decentralization and interest concessions", to reforms in ownership. The course can be generally divided into three stages.

The first stage existed between 1979 and 1986, when the reform on the operation of state-owned enterprises was conducted. The main measures adopted in this period related to "decentralization and interest concessions", "replacement of profit by tax", and "replacement of allocation of funds by loan grants". At the beginning of the reform, the government realized that a serious shortcoming in the traditional planned economy was the inflexible management, so in the reform, the government should provide greater authority to enterprises to enable them to run their own businesses under the guidance of the national unified plan. After the Third Plenary Session of the 11th Central Committee, the central government released a series of documents to expand enterprises' rights to run their own businesses and promote the reform on the operation of state-owned enterprises, with the "decentralization and interest concessions" as the most significant characteristic of the reform of state-owned enterprises in this stage.

However, without the supporting reform of the macro-policy environment and the resource allocation mechanism, a competing market should not be economically reformed, so the government cannot judge the actual operation performance of enterprises through the external operation indicators. On the other hand, the problem of information asymmetry between the government and enterprises has been made worse because of the policy burdens of state-owned enterprises, leading to the moral hazard of managers of state-owned enterprises, who have the motive and ability to invade and usurp profits of the state and may use policy burden as an excuse for the poor management or losses suffered by the enterprises, when such enterprises obtain certain rights of production and management. Therefore, the serious problem of "wages invading profits" emerged during the reform of "decentralization and interest concessions", as the profits of state-owned assets and national financial incomes had not seen a significant growth. In order to guarantee the national financial incomes and strengthen the state-owned enterprises' economic responsibilities and budget constraints, the government had carried out the reform of "replacement of profit by tax" and "replacement of allocation of funds by loan grants", but failed to reach a favorable result.

The second stage of the reform of state-owned enterprises lasted from 1987 to 1992, when the thrust of the reform of gradually moved from enterprises to reform of the ownership. During this period, the main reform measures included the reform of enterprises' "contract system" and the reform of the "shareholding system" that was not fully implemented. The transition from the reform of enterprises to the reform of ownership was inspired by the successful reform of the household contract responsibility system, so the government considered restraining the state-owned enterprises under the original property relation and promoting the reform of the "contract system" for enterprises. Therefore, two rounds of contract system reforms had been applied on state-owned enterprises between 1987 and 1992. The main objective of the contract managerial responsibility system is to guarantee the submission of taxes and profits, and the technical reconstruction and linking of the total sum of wages to the economic benefits of enterprises. In the beginning, the contract system had indeed stimulated the enthusiasm of enterprises and staff and promoted the development of the national economy. However, at the same time, there was a rapid decline in efficiency, economic growth, and the proportion of national financial income in GDP. Actually, the contract system cannot solve moral hazards faced by the managers of state-owned enterprises when the enterprises continued to assume the policy burdens. Firstly, the contract agreement was only responsible for the profits, but not losses, so the managers of state-owned enterprises would impute the losses of enterprises to the policy burdens. Secondly, the contract system also incurred the short-term goal-oriented act within the contracting period, which influenced the long-term healthy development of enterprises and national economy. Some domestic scholars proposed to promote the shareholding system reform in state-owned enterprises. These scholars believed that the goal of the shareholding system reform was to change the state-monopoly enterprise's property system, form a diversified property rights structure within the state-owned enterprises, and thus optimize the internal governance structure of state-owned enterprises and effectively stimulate and restrict shareholders, the board of directors, and executives. A pilot of the shareholding system in state-owned enterprises started in 1986, but it exerted only a small influence since it was carried out mostly in small- and medium-sized state-owned enterprises.

The third stage for the reform of state-owned enterprises lasted from 1992 to the present, when the "modern enterprise system" reform was adopted. Against the problems in the contract system, the Third Plenary Session of the 14th Communist Party of China (CPC) Central Committee established the goal for the reform of state-owned enterprises with the establishment of the "modern enterprise system" and summarized it's

characteristics as "clearly established ownership, well-defined power and
responsibility, separation of enterprise from administration, and scientific management". Immediately following the establishment, the Law
of Corporation was issued in February 1993. Since then, the "modern
enterprise system" has always been the main principle of the reform of
state-owned enterprises in China, especially the large- and medium-sized
state-owned enterprises. However, for large- and medium-sized state-owned
enterprises, even the modern enterprise system cannot solve the existing
problem in the contract managerial responsibility system. The effective
operation of modern company governance structure relies on the market system for fair competition among products, factors, management, and stock,
but the market system has not yet been formed in the Chinese economy.
Since the policy burdens of enterprises continue to exist, moral hazards and
soft budget constraint of state-owned enterprises cannot be eliminated.

1.3. *The root of problems in China's state-owned
enterprises*

The root of the problem of state-owned enterprises lies such enterprises
generally assuming policy burdens, which leads to soft budget constraints
and "viability"[3] of enterprises. Before any conclusions are made, a theoretical review will be conducted on the entrustment and agency problems
in modern enterprises, and then the root problems in China's state-owned
enterprises would be specifically analyzed.

Being the main body of the state-owned enterprises of China, the
large- and medium-sized state-owned enterprises, similar to many modern
enterprises in the west, are faced with the problem of entrustment and
agencies led by the separation of ownership from management. The
agency relationship features three important characteristics: the first is
the information asymmetry where the managers, as the agents, own more
enterprise information than the general enterprise owners; the second is

---

[3] Viability is defined by the estimated profit of an enterprise. If an enterprise is estimated to
earn normal profits accepted by the society in a free, open, and competing market through
normal operation and management, the enterprise possesses the viability, and vice versa. Lin
Yifu (2002). The development strategy. In *Viability and Economic Convergence, Quarterly
Journal of Economics*, 1(2), 2694300.

the incompatible excitation where enterprise managers and owners clash in achieving the goals; and the third is the unequal responsibilities between the managers and owners. Managers often lose much less than the enterprise owners when the enterprise managers make a wrong decision.

During the long years of development, a series of system arrangements has been established in the western countries in order to solve the internal incompatible excitation of enterprise managers led by the agency relationship. The system arrangements can be divided into the "external governance mechanism of the enterprise" and the "internal governance mechanism of the enterprise", where the former aims to release the problem of information asymmetry between managers and owners, and the latter mainly aims to overcome the problems of internal incompatible excitation and unequal responsibilities. The breakthrough point of the solution to the agency problem is to solve the problem in the external governance mechanism of the enterprise, because the internal problems of the incompatible excitation and unequal responsibilities can only be settled when the information asymmetry is released. The internal excitation problem cannot be solved based only on the adjustment of the internal governance structure of the enterprise — the problem in the external governance mechanism should be solved firstly.

The external governance mechanism of the enterprise mainly includes an open, fair, and competing market for products and factors, and managers and stock. The main function of the external system arrangements is to release the problem of information asymmetry between enterprise owners and managers, because many external performance indicators, such as the profit ratio and stock prices, are closely related to the enterprises' understanding and efforts in a fair, open, and competitive market. These indicators reveal the information, which can be regarded as the information basis for enterprise owners to improve the internal governance structure of their enterprises. The functions of the internal governance structure include the following: firstly, to design the best contract for enterprise managers according to the indicators provided by the external market. Secondly, to ensure the correctness of major decisions through a clear procedure and lower the potential damages brought about by unequal responsibilities. Therefore, improvements in the internal governance structure cannot be realized without the external governance mechanism that can accurately reflect the information. The open, fair, and competitive market is the only form of the enterprise's external governance mechanism, while the internal governance mechanisms may vary in different countries and enterprises.

China concentrated mainly on the heavy industry, thus leading to the rise of many state-owned enterprises in China. Therefore, the state-owned enterprises in China were distinguished from general enterprises under the free market economy for their policy burdens. The policy burdens of the state-owned enterprises can be divided into social and strategic policy burdens. The social policy burdens refer to the burdens incurred by the state-owned enterprises that assume too many social functions, such as excess personnel, retirement pay of workers, and endowment insurance. The strategic policy burdens refer to the burdens led by state-owned enterprises investing in relatively capital-intensive industries and industrial sections that China has no comparative advantages in, under the guidance of the traditional development strategy.[4] The agency problem of state-owned enterprises that bear the policy burdens is also featured with three characteristics mentioned earlier. For example, regarding the incompatible excitation, the government requires the state-owned enterprises to implement its catching-up strategy and to assume the policy burdens, but it is the enterprise managers who reap the maximum profits.

As mentioned earlier, an effective external governance mechanism is the precondition for the success of the enterprise reform, but it cannot be realized when enterprises are still bearing the policy burdens. China failed, during the earlier reform process of state-owned enterprises, mainly because it not only ignored the most important reform of the external governance mechanism but also adjusted the internal governance structure. For example, the reform of "decentralization and interest concessions" and "contract system" mainly aimed to stimulate the enthusiasm of the managers and workers of state-owned enterprises and increase the value of state-owned

---

[4] See details of this topic in Lin Yifu, Cai Chuang and Li Zhou (1997). *Full Information and Reform of State-Owned Enterprises*. Shanghai Sanlian Bookstore: Shanghai People Publishing House; Lin Yifu, Cai Chuang and Li Zhou (1999). *China's Miracle: Development Strategies and Economic Reform*, enlarged Ed. Shanghai Sanlian Bookstore; and Lin Yifu and Liu Peilin (2001). Eliminating policy burdens, improving the viability of enterprises and creating a new situation for the reform of state-owned enterprises in the 10th Five-Year Plan. *Newsletter of the China Center for Economic Research of Beijing University*, (38).

assets. However, as the information asymmetry had not been released when the enterprises were still bearing the policy burdens and the external macro environment was still distorted, the simple reform of "decentralization and interest concessions" and "contract system" would only aggravate the moral hazards of managers in the state-owned enterprises. The reform of state-owned enterprises from 1992 to the present placed tremendous efforts to establish the modern enterprise system, with the theoretical logic that the uncomfortable situation of the reform lay in the unclear ownership, irrational internal governance structure of the enterprise, and weak management.[5] Actually, it is unwarranted to blame the problems of state-owned enterprises on the unclear ownership of state-owned enterprises, because there is no legal ambiguity that state-owned enterprises are owned by all the people in China. Based on the comparison between Chinese state-owned enterprises and the large- and medium-sized enterprises of the developed countries in the west, the difference does not exist in the number of owners, but in the external governance mechanism that can effectively reveal information. The most typical example is the former Soviet Union and East European countries. They had reached the critical point in property rights reform as part of their privatization reform, but, as known to all, the efficiency of their enterprises after the reform continues to be very low.

The elimination of policy burdens for state-owned enterprises is the precondition to build an effective external governance mechanism that can accurately reveal information. If the policy burdens remain in state-owned enterprises, the information asymmetry between the government and enterprise managers cannot be solved, even though an open and competing market exists, which would also lead to the soft budget constraint of enterprises.[6] This is because the state-owned enterprises with policy burdens lack viability, so they would incur losses in a competitive market. The government is bonded to the losses incurred by the policy burdens, but, owing to information asymmetry, the government cannot predict the

---

[5] Wu Jinglian (1994). *Modern Companies and Enterprise Reform*. Tianjin: Tianjin People's Press.

[6] Lin, Justin Yifu, Cai, Fang and Li, Zhou (1998). Competition, policy burdens, and state-owned enterprises reform. *American Economic Review*, 88(2), 422–427; Lin, Justin Yifu and Tan, Guofu (1999). Policy burdens, accountability, and soft budget constraint. *America Economic Review*, 89(2), 426–431.

magnitude of losses incurred on account of policy burdens and those brought about by the weak management of enterprises. The enterprise managers impute all losses to the policy burden. When the government cannot tell the difference between the two kinds of losses and cannot deny its responsibility to the losses incurred by policy burdens, it has to provide subsidies after the enterprise losses are formed, leading to the emergence of the "soft budget constraint". The moral hazard of state-owned enterprises' managers would be aggravated because of the estimated soft budget constraint.

As long as the enterprises bear the policy burdens, the enterprises cannot eliminate the problem of the soft budget constraint. Whether the enterprises bear the policy burdens has nothing to do with the pattern of ownership of enterprises, so there is no necessary relation between the soft budget constraint and the ownership of enterprises.[7] Several different situations are summarized as follows: (i) Even though the developed countries in the west have established perfect market and legal systems, when the enterprises are bearing policy burdens, the governments have to provide subsidies to the enterprise's losses, leading to the low efficiency among enterprises. The typical example is the British government that protects the coal mining industry, which lacks comparative advantage and viability. (ii) In the developing countries, with private economy as the main body, when the enterprises are required to catch up and surpass the advanced level set by the governments, there also exists the problem of the soft budget constraint. A typical example is of South Korea that provided the subsidy of soft budget constraint to large enterprises for the development of heavy machinery and heavy and chemical industry in the 1970s. (iii) For transforming countries that had conducted the reform of privatization in a radical way, enterprises are receiving even more subsidies after the reform, which demonstrates that privatization cannot solve the problem of the soft budget constraint.

The above statements do not mean to exclude the change of ownership, but states that the elimination of policy burdens is the precondition for the successful reform of the state-owned enterprises. According to the economic environment, enterprises and other micro-market subjects should

---

[7]Lin Yifu and Li Zhibin (2004). Policy burden, moral hazard and soft budget constraint. *Economic Research*, (2).

decide whether the ownership be changed after the elimination of policy burdens. The government should not simply promote or prohibit ownership changes in enterprises. In addition, if some enterprises decide to change their ownership, the state-owned assets, including the land and intangible assets, should be sold at the market price, and the realization of such sale should be utilized to pay for the government's debt in the social security funds, and so on.

2. The Structure of China's Financial System

2.1. *Overview of China's financial system*

Fundamentally, the financial system was established and developed to serve the real economy by mobilizing the idle social funds and effectively allocating them to production departments or individuals that need funds. Since the late 1970s, the restoration and development of China's financial system has been closely related to the reform and development of the real economy, especially the reform of state-owned enterprises. After more than two decades of development, China has had good results in the development of the financial system, despite some serious system problems. The relatively complete financial system, with banks as the main body, has taken shape.

According to the absolute statistical indicators, China's financial system is extremely large in size. By the end of 2002, the balance of China's broad money (M2) had reached 18.5 trillion yuan, which equaled 180% of GDP of that year. At the same time, the number of listed companies in the two stock exchanges in Shanghai and Shenzhen had reached 1,224, with a total stock value of 3.83 trillion yuan, which equaled 37.4% of GDP of that year, including 1.25 trillion yuan of the total value of trade. By the end of 2002, the balance of bonds amounted to 3.07 trillion yuan, taking up 30% of GDP, but most of them were national debts and financial bonds released by the central government and policy banks, and only a few belonged to enterprise bonds.[8] By April 2002, the total assets of all financial institutions in China had exceeded 22.5 trillion yuan, approximately equaling 240% of GDP,

---

[8]Here, the statistics of bonds do not include the bonds that were released by the four asset management corporations and held by the four major state-owned commercial banks.

including 21.3 trillion yuan of the assets of financial institutions under the supervision of the people's bank, 654 billion yuan of the assets of securities companies, and 514.1 billion yuan of the assets of the insurance companies.[9]

Undoubtedly, banks are the core and main body of the current financial system of China. By the end of 2001, the total assets of banks had reached 19.1 trillion yuan, the deposit balance had amounted to 13.9 trillion yuan, and the loan balance had reached 11.5 trillion yuan. The state-owned commercial banks, policy banks, and shareholding commercial banks that occupy about 90% market share of all financial organizations are directly or indirectly owned or share-held by the government. Financial organizations, other than banks, mainly include insurance, funds, and securities companies. By the end of 2001, there were about 59 insurance companies, with a total asset amounting to 459 billion yuan; the assets of funds companies only amounted to more than 100 billion yuan; and more than 110 securities companies had been established, with a total asset amount of 654 billion yuan.

The structure of China's financial system can also be reviewed from an international aspect. The financial assets and size of GDP of different countries in 2000, as well as the ratio of the two, are summarized in Table 9.3, which reflects the proportion of financial intermediaries (banks) and capital market in the financial system. It shows that cash and deposits (M2) have occupied most shares in the financial capitals held by the residents and enterprises in China, almost equal to two times that of security assets (194%). The proportion is almost higher than all developed countries, compared to 67%, 59%, and 21% of Germany, Japan, and America, respectively. Without a doubt, banks dominate the financial system in China.

Significant characteristics can be discovered from Table 9.3. One characteristic is that developing countries of lower per-capita GDP share a higher proportion of M2 and security capital, which indicate that in these countries, banks play a major role in the financial systems, but developed countries see a lower proportion in this aspect. In other words, the financial market plays a more important role in the financial system of the developed countries than most developing countries. Actually, at the initial stages of economic development, enterprises of most industries are

---

[9]Dai Xianglong (2002). On main problems in China's financial reform. *Journals of the Central University of Finance and Economics*, (8).

Table 9.3. International Comparison of the Financial Scale and Financial Structure (2000) (Unit: U.S. Dollars).

Country or region	Money M2	Capital of financial market			Proportion in GDP (%)			M2/(stock+bonds) (%)	Per-capita GDP (US$1,000)
		Stock	Bonds	GDP	M2	Stock	Bonds		
Thailand	123 billion	29 billion		116 billion	106	25		420	1.9
China	1.626 trillion	581 billion	257 billion	1.066 trillion	153	55	24	194	0.9
India	250 billion	25 billion	133 billion	449 billion	56		30	189	0.5
Philippines	41 billion			66 billion	63	38		164	1
Portugal	116 billion	61 billion	65 billion	107 billion	109	57	61	93	10.4
South Korea	327 billion	148 billion	269 billion	409 billion	80	36	66	78	9.7
Argentina	91 billion	46 billion	85 billion	285 billion	32	16	30	69	7.7
Turkey	84 billion	70 billion	55 billion	189 billion	45	37	29	68	2.8
Germany	1.986 trillion	1.270 trillion	1.689 trillion	1.899 trillion	105	67	89	67	22.8
Spain	539 billion	504 billion	331 billion	567 billion	95	89	58	65	14.2
Mexico	120 billion	125 billion	69 billion	568 billion	21	22	12	62	5.9
Japan	5,480	3.194 trillion	6.078 trillion	4,455	123	72	136	59	36.8
Chinese Hong Kong	385 billion	623 billion	41 billion	163 billion	237	384	25	58	23.3
Chile	33 billion	60 billion		66 billion	50	92		54	4.3
Singapore	99 billion	155 billion	29 billion	92 billion	108	169	32	54	23.1
South Africa	66 billion	131 billion		115 billion	57	114		50	2.9
Malaysia	92 billion	113 billion	76 billion	89 billion	103	127	85	49	3.9

(Continued)

Table 9.3. (*Continued*)

Country or region	Money M2	Capital of financial market			Proportion in GDP (%)			M2/(stock+ bonds) (%)	Per-capita GDP (US$1,000)
		Stock	Bonds	GDP	M2	Stock	Bonds		
Belgium	238 billion	183 billion	318 billion	230 billion	103	79	138	48	0
Australia	248 billion	373 billion	172 billion	363 billion	68	103	47	46	20.7
Britain	1.550 trillion	2.612 trillion	897 billion	1.395 trillion	111	187	64	44	23.6
France	910 billion	1.447 trillion	1.068 trillion	1.313 trillion	69	110	81	36	21.8
Switzerland	324 billion	792 billion	163 billion	249 billion	130	318	66	34	34.3
Canada	447 billion	780 billion	589 billion	704 billion	64	111	84	33	22.2
Italy	637 billion	768 billion	1.272 trillion	1.090 trillion	59	71	117	31	18.4
Brazil	161 billion	226 billion	293 billion	558 billion	29	41	53	31	3.5
America	6.081 trillion	15.215 trillion	14.466 trillion	9.873 trillion	62	154	147	21	35
Sweden	95 billion	328 billion	197 billion	218 billion	44	150	90	18	25.3
Finland	60 billion	294 billion	68 billion	123 billion	49	239	55	17	24
Holland	0	641 billion	341 billion	375 billion	0	171	91	0	22.8

Source: M2: IFM; Stock: FIBV Table 1.3; bonds: domestic debt securities, BIS.

small in size and demand fewer capitals, and the information disclosure and market supervision systems are imperfect. This inhibits enterprises from adopting the direct external financing method, so indirect financing becomes the main financing channel of these enterprises.[10] Along with economic development, some large enterprises of large scale and high standing would emerge, and the information and supervision systems would be improved constantly, so it would become possible for more enterprises to employ direct financing. Therefore, along with economic development, banks would play a weaker role in enterprise financing, but they are essential for economic development at the starting period.

Aside from financial assets, China's financial system can also be analyzed from the perspective of corporate finance. Table 9.4 shows the statistics of the channels for external financing of enterprises, which reflect the dominant position of bank credit among the external financing methods for Chinese enterprises. The loan financing accounted for 88.9%, stock financing had taken up 8.6%, and the bond financing had occupied only 0.5% of the total external financing of enterprises from 1996 to 2001.

2.2. The course of China's financial reform

Despite its capital scarcity, China has adopted the strategy to prioritize the development of heavy industry since the 1950s. In order to allocate at least limited amounts of capital to the heavy industry, which in reality requires large investments, the government operated a monopoly of the financial system and conducted a highly concentrated planned management.[11] Correspondingly, after the foundation of New China, the People's Bank of China in the Ministry of Finance took over the financial organizations. The People's Bank functioned as the financial management center of the country and was meanwhile involved in credit businesses, so a unified financial

---

[10] See more details of the discussion on the characteristics of direct and indirect financing in: Lin Yifu and Li Yongjun (2001). Development of medium and small-sized financial institutions and financing of medium and small-sized enterprises. *Economic Research*, (1).

[11] See more details in: Lin Yifu (1999). Outlook of Chinese economy of the new millennium. In *Studies of Chinese Economy*, Lin Yifu, Hai Wen and Ping Xinqiao (eds.). Beijing: Beijing University Press; Lin Yifu (1999). What is the direction for China's reform of financial system. In *China: Economic Transformation and Economic Policies*, Hai Wen and Lu Feng (eds.). Beijing: Beijing University Press.

Table 9.4. External Financing Structure of Chinese Enterprises (Unit: Trillion Yuan).

Year	Total financing amount	RMB and foreign currency loans		Stock financing		Paper financing		Bond financing	
		Increase	Proportion (%)	Increase	Proportion (%)	Increase	Proportion (%)	Increase	Proportion (%)
1996	1.158	1.114	96.2	42.5	3.7	6.4	0.5	−4.9	−0.4
1997	1.2583	1.140	90.6	128.5	10.2	−2.5	−0.2	−7.7	−0.6
1998	1.2814	1.152	89.9	84	6.5	29.4	2.3	16	1.3
1999	1.2076	1.0721	88.8	94.1	7.8	29.4	2.4	10.2	1
2000	1.5872	1.2887	81.2	210.4	13.3	79.8	5	8.3	0.5
2001	1.4016	1.2524	89.4	116.9	8.3	17.6	1.3	14.7	1
Total	7.8941	7.0192	88.9	676.4	8.6	160.1	2.0	36.6	0.5

[1]The RMB and foreign currency loans, paper financing, and bond financing of financial organizations refer to the newly increased balance of that year.

[2]The amount of RMB and foreign currency loans includes the allotment of shares and convertible bonds financing.

[3]The financing amount of the commercial bills equals the ending balance of newly increased banker's acceptance, minus newly increased balance of the bank discount, because the bank discount has been already counted in the loans of financial organizations as the indirect financing.

[4]The foreign currencies are converted to RMB based on the average exchange rate of that year.

[5]The bonds financing of 2001 refer to the amount of bonds circulation, since the balance has not been calculated.

Source: Wu Jinglian (2002). Reform of banks: the most important of the financing reform. *World Economic Papers*, (4). The last row was calculated by the author.

system was formed to support the catching-up and surpassing strategies. Along with the implementation of the reform and opening up since the late 1970s, the traditional, highly concentrated planned economy system had been broken up, development of a real economy was initiated, and China's financial system was reconstructed and constantly improved toward the market system to support reform measures that were constantly deepening. Some important aspects of China's financial reform are briefly reviewed here.[12]

2.2.1. *The reform of banks*

Along with the execution of economic reform, some economic surpluses were gradually transferred into families, and enterprises increasingly held their autonomy in management, which necessitated China's financial services to be restored. From 1979 to 1984, China had restored and established several wholly state-owned banks, including the Agricultural Bank of China, China Construction Bank, China Investment Bank, and the Industrial and Commercial Bank of China. Bank of China was transformed into a bank specializing in the business of exchange rate. All these banks were specialized and specific operation ranges, and had no overlapping businesses. After 1985, the central government began to establish share-holding commercial banks according to the principle of market operation, based on the requirements for financial services in the development of national economy on, including nationwide or regional commercial banks, such as the Bank of Communications, CITIC Industrial Bank, and Huaxia Bank. At the same time, the government started to transform the specialized banks into commercial banks and allowed enterprises to become involved in comprehensive businesses. Therefore, a cross competition among banks emerged, which initially laid the foundation for the commercialization of banks.

State-owned specialized banks are bearing policy loans at different degrees, which lead to a large amount of non-performing assets in these banks. In order to improve the status, the government founded three policy

[12]See more information on the course of China's financial reform: Lin Yifu, Li Zhibin, *Reform of Chinese State-Owned Enterprises and Financial System*, No C2003027 exposure draft of China Center for Economic Research of Beijing University, 2003.

banks in 1994 (the State Development Bank, the Export and Import Bank of China, and the Agriculture Development Bank of China), to assume the policy credit business that was originally managed by specialized banks. After the Law of Commercial Banks of China was enforced in 1995, the commercialization of the four state-owned specialized banks officially began.[13] However, the huge volumes of non-performing assets that had been accumulated for a long time incurred high financial risks for banks. The Asian financial crisis that broke out in 1997 strengthened the central government's determination to eradicate the banks' non-performing assets. In 1998, the government had issued a special national debt of 270 billion yuan to state-owned commercial banks to supplement their capital. Four major asset management companies set up in succession during 1999 to 2000 had removed the non-performing assets of 1.4 trillion yuan from the four state-owned banks. In addition to this, in 1998, the State Council asked the state-owned commercial banks to reduce the number of branches and downsize staff strength. It also lowered the ratio of non-performing loans to 2%–3% every year, in order to reduce the operation losses of the state-owned commercial banks. Subsequently, the four state-owned commercial banks were dismantled and most branches were merged at lower than the county level (except the Agricultural Bank of China). Thus, bank businesses started to concentrate in central cities.

2.2.2. *The reform of the capital market*

With the deepening of reform and implementation in the shareholding system of state-owned enterprises, the scale of stock issuance started to increase. In addition to the general RMB A-share, the special B-share of foreign currencies and the H-share released in Hong Kong were issued in succession after 1991. The foundation of the Shanghai and Shenzhen stock exchanges in 1990 and 1991, respectively, symbolized the formation of the concentrated stock trading market in China. At first, the "quota system" was adopted for listing Chinese enterprises. Such enterprises were recommended by provincial governments, so most listed companies were state-owned enterprises of poor quality, which led to the problem of "rent-seeking" in the listing process. After the Securities Law was issued in 1999, the

---

[13]The China Investment Bank had been incorporated into the State Development Bank in March 1999.

"quota system" was replaced by the "approval system", which required the securities organizations to examine companies applying for listing and recommend them to the China Securities Regulatory Commission (CSRC) based on the results of examination, and required the CSRC to finally determine whether the company could become listed. Under the new system, the quality of the listed companies was improved and the proportion of non-state-owned enterprises was increased. However, there still exists many serious systemic problems in the stock markets of China.

During the early stages of the reform, investments in state-owned enterprises and construction of infrastructure mostly relied on financial appropriation, which constantly increased the financial deficit. In 1981, China had restored the release of national debts which had actually been stopped 23 years ago and established a system for the annual issuance of treasury notes. However, before 1990, the release of national debts mainly relied on political mobilization and administrative distribution. Since 1991, the underwriting method has been applied in issuing national debts, and the primary and secondary markets for the release of national debts were formed in this period. In 1994, reforms were carried out in the financial system to prevent finance from overdraft on banks. So, the financial deficit was resolved by releasing the national debts. A series of reform measures have been adopted in the national debts market since 1994, and a comparatively complete national debt market has been formed. The issuance of financial bonds in China has made great progress. After 1994, the policy financial bonds that were issued by the policy banks gradually became the main part of China's financial bonds. However, the market of enterprise bonds in China remained stagnant for a long time. By the end of 2001, the balance of issued enterprise bonds only accounted for 4% of the total balance of bonds market. The balances of national debts and policy financial bonds took up 62% and 34%, respectively.

2.2.3. *The reform of the financial supervision system*

Although the State Council had initially confirmed the role of the People's Bank as the central bank as early as 1983, it truly functioned as an independent central bank only from 1993. The release of the Law pertaining to the People's Bank of China in 1995 symbolized that the role and responsibilities of the People's Bank of China as the central bank had been confirmed in legal form. In 1998, the People's Bank of China carried out major reforms in its management system, including dissolving the provincial branches of the People's Bank and setting up regional branches for several provinces (autonomous regions and municipalities directly under the central government) in order to enhance the independence of the People's Bank. In terms of monetary policies, the People's Bank of China established the monetary policy committee in March 1997. The People's Bank of China transformed its monetary policy measure from the direct control of loan scale to the adjustment of the base money by utilizing several monetary policy instruments.

As guided by the general thought of "segregated operation and supervision", the function of supervising the securities and insurance industry was isolated from the People's Bank of China. In October 1992, the CSRC was founded to supervise the securities sector. In November 1998, the China Insurance Regulatory Commission was established to supervise the insurance sector. In March 2003, the China Banking Regulatory Commission was established upon approval by the National People's Congress to supervise banking financial organizations and to separate the supervision function from the People's Bank. It was agreed that the People's Bank of China would be responsible for the formulation and implementation of monetary policies as an independent central bank. The frame of the "segregated supervision" of China's financial system was thus established.

2.3. *Main problems of China's financial system*

Objectively speaking, in over two decades, China's financial system has made great achievements in many aspects through reform and development. However, as an important part of the entire economic system reform, the financial reform is essentially affected by the reforms in real economy, especially the reform of the state-owned enterprises, which leads to many serious problems in the financial system. In this section, the main problems of China's financial system are briefly reviewed.

2.3.1. *Huge amount of non-performing assets of the banking system*

In March 2002, Dai Xianglong, the president of the People's Bank of China, announced at the China Development High-Level Forum that the ratio of the non-performing loans of the state-owned commercial banks was 25.37%

by the end of 2001. Based on this, the balance of non-performing loans of state-owned commercial banks amounted to 2.3 trillion yuan. However, in 2000, the four major capital management companies had removed 1.4 trillion yuan of non-performing assets from the state-owned commercial banks. The state-owned commercial enterprises took up 63% of total assets of the banking industry in China, which reflected the severity of the problem of non-performing assets in the banking system.

In addition to the state-owned commercial banks, the high rate of non-performing loans also exists in other financial organizations in the banking system, where the problem is even more serious. The bank-run crisis had broken out in many urban and rural credit cooperatives in the late 1990s, adversely reflecting social stability. The People's Bank of China focused on the governance of credit cooperatives and shut down many small- and medium-sized financial organizations. It was estimated that the non-performing assets rate of the rural credit cooperatives had generally exceeded 60% with a very low asset quality. The same problem also exists in policy banks. The return rate of policy loans is generally very low, and the policy banks collect funds for loans by issuing the policy financial bonds, which are mainly purchased by state-owned commercial banks. Therefore, the policy loans are only removed from the state-owned enterprises in paper, but in reality, the state-owned commercial banks continue to bear the losses and risks of the policy loans.

The four major capital management companies that were established in 1999 and 2000 showed unsatisfactory performance in disposal and recovery of non-performing assets. According to the research conducted by the Bank for International Settlements, the capital recovered from the disposal of non-performing assets by these capital management companies in the past couple of years are not sufficient to pay the interests of the bonds from the assets management companies that are held by the four major commercial banks.[14] Therefore, no promising prospects can be seen to deal with the non-performing assets of banks by establishing asset management companies.

As shown in Table 9.5, the scale of the non-performing assets in China's banking industry can be roughly estimated conservatively. It is estimated that the total loss incurred by the non-performing assets in China's banking

---

[14] Ma, Guonan and Fung, Ben (2002). China's asset management corporations. BIS Working Papers No. 115.

Table 9.5. Estimations of the Scale of Non-Performing Loans in China's Banking Industry and Losses Incurred (2001) (Unit: Yuan).

	Loan balance	Rate of non-performing loans (%)	Amount of non-performing loans	Rate of the loss of non-performing loans (%)	Total loss	Total loss/GDP (%)
State-owned commercial banks	7.058 trillion	25	1.7645 trillion	50	882.25 billion	9.2
Shareholding commercial banks	1.054 trillion	10	105.4 billion	50	52.7 billion	0.5
Rural credit cooperatives	1.274 trillion	50	637 billion	50	318.5 billion	3.3
Urban credit cooperatives	550 billion	40	220 billion	50	110 billion	1.1
Policy banks	1.571 trillion	40	628.4 billion	50	314.2 billion	3.3
Subtotal	11.507 trillion	—	3.3553 trillion	—	1.67765 trillion	17.5
Asset management cooperation	1.400 trillion	100	1.400 trillion	80	1.120 trillion	11.7
Total	12.907 trillion	—	4.7553 trillion	—	2.79765 trillion	29.2

Source: Almanac of China's Finance and Banking (2002).

system by the end of 2001 amounted to 2.8 trillion yuan, accounting for 29.2% of GDP, compared to the total financial incomes of China in 2001, which equaled 1.64 trillion yuan, accounting for only 17.1% of GDP. Therefore, the huge amount of non-performing assets is undoubtedly a heavy burden in the economic development of China.

2.3.2. *Highly concentrated market structure of the banking industry*

The banking industry in China is so highly concentrated that the assets, deposits, and loans of the four major state-owned commercial banks equals 63%, 70%, and 61%, respectively. The high concentration of the banking industry and the lack of small- and medium-sized banks that serve small- and medium-sized enterprises have led to difficulties in financing the small- and medium-sized enterprises. Take the township enterprises as an example. Most township enterprises are small and medium sized. The value of Chinese township enterprises in 2001 had increased to 3.2386 trillion yuan, accounting for 34.3% of GDP, but only obtained 5.7% of the total loans of the society.

Most small- and medium-sized enterprises realize external financing through bank loans. Large banks are faced with "high cost, difficult mortgage, and big risk" for loans provided to small- and medium-sized enterprises owing to factors such as high concentration of China's banking industry, small loan scale for small- and medium-sized enterprises, serious information asymmetry and lack of enough mortgage credit. Compared to the large banks, small- and medium-sized financial organizations are more willing to provide financial services to small- and medium-sized enterprises, because they cannot do so for large enterprises owing to lack of capital. Small- and medium-sized financial organizations hold advantages in information and cost for the service for small- and medium-sized enterprises, and they bear lower transaction costs owing to the fewer management levels and flexible management practices. An effective method to resolve the difficulties in securing finance for small- and medium-sized enterprises is to develop small- and medium-sized financial organizations, and private banks.[15]

2.3.3. *Distorted stock market*

Most listed companies in China are state-owned enterprises, while the number of non-state-owned enterprises only takes up 7%, which is the result of governmental policies. Originally, the government aimed to create conditions for the reform and financing of state-owned enterprises by establishing the stock market. The low quality of listed companies is one major characteristic of the Chinese stock market, because, as guided by the original "quota system", local governments often recommend state-owned enterprises of low quality requiring capital to go public, whereas the high quality enterprises mostly do not go public. Other characteristics of the Chinese stock market include the following: 70% of stocks, as state-owned shares and corporate shares, are not involved in circulation, and the floating stock takes up only 30% of stock value; the speculation on the stock market is very serious that the average turnover rate of Shanghai and Shenzhen stock exchanges in the eight years between 1994 and 2001 reached 504.7%, which means that the turnover rate is five times a year, compared to 67.1% of the New York stock market and 40% of Tokyo[16]; and the price/earnings rate of stocks is very high, approaching 40% in Shanghai and Shenzhen stock market in 2001, compared to about 8.5% in Hong Kong. In addition, the trends in the Chinese stock market have no close resemblance to the performance of the real economy, as shown in Fig. 9.2.

2.3.4. *Lack of enterprise bonds market*

The enterprise bonds market is lacking in China. By the end of 2001, the balance of enterprise bonds issued occupied only 4% of the total balance of market bonds (see Fig. 9.3). The scale of enterprise bonds cannot be

---

[15]Lin Yifu, Li Yongjun (2001). Development of small and medium financial organizations and financing of small and medium-sized enterprises. *Economic Research*, (1).

[16]Lin Yifu (2001). Four problems on Chinese stock market. *Newsletter of the China Center for Economic Research of Beijing University*. (7).

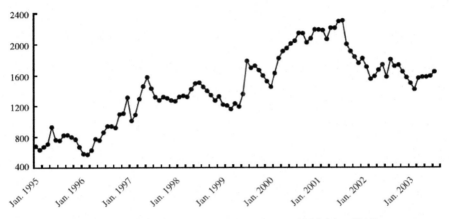

Figure 9.2.   Shanghai A-Share Index (January 1995–May 2003).
Source: The website of the China's Securities Regulatory Commission.

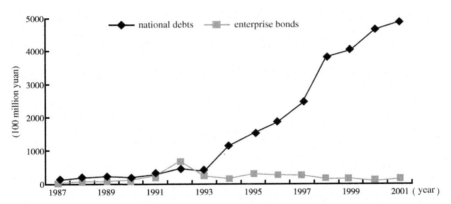

Figure 9.3. Annual Issuance Amount of National Debts and Enterprise Bonds (1987–2001).
Source: *China Securities and Futures Statistical Yearbook* (2001) and the *Almanac of China's Finance* (2002).

compared to the newly increased yearly loans of banks. Enterprise bonds often take up about 30% of total external financing in countries with a mature market economy, only second to the bank loans.[17] Two reasons can

----

[17]Frederic Mishkin (1998). *Monetary Finance*. China: Renmin University Press.

be summarized for the stagnancy of the bonds market in China. Firstly, the financial laws and regulations in China are not completely sound. The illegal fund collection was often seen in the late 1980s and early 1990s, leading to social unrest due to the incapability to repay loans on time, so the central government strengthened its control over the issuance of enterprise bonds.[18] Secondly, the government wants to control the financial resources of the society, because the issuance of enterprise bonds would affect the financing plan of national debts. For large-scale, state-owned enterprises that are qualified to issue bonds, they would not be motivated to issue enterprise bonds if they can collect funds from the stock market or bank loans, because the issuance of enterprise bonds is the hardest financing method owing to budget constraints.

2.3.5. *The financial supervision system in urgent demand of improvement*

As the China Banking Regulatory Commission was established upon the approval of the National People's Congress in March 2003, the financial supervision frame of "segregated supervision" of China's financial system has been initially established. Since China's supervision system is at the starting stage and a new situation would emerge after her entry into the WTO, many problems may arise in China's financial supervision. Firstly, the financial laws and regulations are incomplete, and some clauses in the current financial laws do not accord to the new requirements of financial supervision, so the new financial laws and regulations should be gradually formulated. Secondly, the supervision method is still backward. Currently, the administrative supervision is adopted without the supervision focus. Thirdly, the relationships in financial supervision have not been fully rationalized, leading to the lack of efficient coordination and cooperation.

---

[18]The issuance of enterprise bonds was controlled by the People's Bank in the mid-1980s. Later, the power was transferred to provincial governments. Local governments often approved the issuance plan of enterprise bonds for state-owned enterprises that had a close relation with the government, instead of the qualified enterprises for the bonds issuance. Therefore, social unrest took place since the large amount of enterprise bonds could not be returned. The central government centralized the power again in 1993 that required the State Planning Commission to examine and approve the issuance of the enterprise bonds.

In addition, information about financial organizations is not transparent, which inhibits the supervision departments from analyzing and discovering problems.

2.4. *Roots of the problems in China's financial system*

In the previous 20 years, each step of the reconstruction, development, and reform of China's financial system was closely related to the reform of other economic departments. The roots of the problems of the financial system were derived from the roots of the problems in the reform of real economy (particularly state-owned enterprises). With the initiation of reform and opening up since the late 1970s, the government could no longer control economic surpluses and so the demands of the enterprises and individuals on the financial services stimulated the reconstruction of China's financial system. However, the policy burdens assumed by the state-owned enterprises have turned from tacit to explicit, along with the market-oriented reform, and the government is now responsible for the losses of state-owned enterprises incurred by policy burdens. The government has provided "subsidies" to state-owned enterprises in the form of financial subsidies, bank loans, and through successively listing state-owned enterprises. In order to control the financial resources of the entire society, the government would inevitably hold a monopoly over the financial system, which would lead to a high concentration in China's financial sector. Mainly, bank loans are given to state-owned enterprises and most listed companies in the stock market are state-owned enterprises. In addition, in order to utilize the financial resources to provide subsidies to state-owned enterprises, the government has to artificially lower the prices of financial products, including the interest rate of banks and the price/earnings rate of the stock market. Therefore, it is difficult to thoroughly carry out the reform of market-set prices for financial products in China. A detailed analysis is provided in the following subsections.

2.4.1. *The root for the problem of non-performing loans in the banking system*

The large amount of non-performing loans in the banking system is undoubtedly closely related to state-owned enterprises. At the start of the reform, the investment on the production and construction of state-owned enterprises mainly came from financial appropriation of the central government. Along with the gradual restoration of the banking system, the central government adopted the reform of "allocation of funds replaced by loan grants" in order to ease the financial burden and fix the budget constraint of state-owned enterprises, but it failed since state-owned enterprises were still bearing the strategic and social policy burdens. As discussed earlier, the problem of information asymmetry cannot be eased as long as the state-owned enterprises continue to bear the policy burdens. Under these circumstances, managers of state-owned enterprises would blame the policy burdens for the losses. The government could neither tell whether and how much losses were incurred by the policy burdens nor allow the enterprises to shutdown owing to the ideology and social pressure. As a result of this, the government utilized state-owned banks to provide loans to state-owned enterprises, thus leading to the soft budget constraint of state-owned enterprises. Therefore, after a long period of time, a huge amount of non-performing assets was formed in China's banking system. It can be seen that if the government does not remove the policy burdens from state-owned enterprises and if it continues to control the banking system to provide loans for state-owned enterprises, then the problem of non-performing loans in the banking system cannot be solved completely, and the potential risks in China's financial system would grow continuously.

2.4.2. *The root for the high concentration of the banking structure*

The financial resources of the entire banking industry in China have been occupied, approximately 70%, by four major state-owned commercial banks and so the banking industry in China is very highly concentrated. Only a small amount of banks exist in China. Besides the more than 100 urban commercial banks available in different cities, China has only 14 formal shareholding commercial banks.

A historical origin can be found for China's highly concentrated banking structure. In the 1950s, China had begun to prioritize the development of heavy industry, which violated China's comparative advantage. In order to mobilize social capital for the heavy industry and guarantee the survival of enterprises without "viability", the government had to hold monopoly in the financial system, so only one formal financial organization, the People's Bank, was established before the reform. Since the reform and opening up, though banks have been gradually restored, China formed a highly concentrated banking industry based on the establishment of the four major state-owned enterprises to serve large enterprises in order to guarantee the capital demands of state-owned enterprises, as well as the strict limited-access policy in order to control its financial resources.

2.4.3. *Reasons for the system defects of the capital market*

Problems in China's stock market are largely related to the lack of "viability" of most listed companies. China's stock market was established in 1991, to support reforms in state-owned enterprises, which generally bore the social and strategic policy burdens. Although the state holding parent company had removed the problems of excess personnel and pension from the listed subsidiary company before listing, the listed enterprises were unable to constantly provide dividends to shareholders in the competing market, since the strategic burden (the lack of "viability") was not solved. Moreover, the state holding parent companies often illegally appropriated capital financed from the stock market and the operation incomes after the listing of enterprises, so the goal of many state-owned enterprises was to "collect money" this way. As the listed companies generally could not obtain common profits and lacked "viability", it was impossible for the investors to obtain profits from long-term holding stocks; therefore, a large number of short-term speculations appeared. The funds also faced the same problem. However, owing to the huge amounts of capital and small proportion of the circulating shares of listed companies, funds share the opportunity to illegally earn huge profits by controlling the stock prices. These are the direct reasons for the prevailing speculations and the fierce fluctuations in the stock market.

3. Direction of the Reform of the State-Owned Enterprises and Financial System in China

3.1. *Direction of the reform of the state-owned enterprises*

According to the analysis provided earlier, the root of the problem in state-owned enterprises is related to soft budget constraints and lack of "viability" incurred by the policy burden. The previous reforms in state-owned enterprises were aimed at the internal governance structure of enterprises, such as the reforms of the "contract system" and "shareholding system", but ignored the external governance mechanism, which was, in fact, the precondition for the success of the internal system reform. However, the precondition to establish the external governance system and relieve the information asymmetry was to remove the policy burdens of state-owned enterprises and solve the problem of the viability of state-owned enterprises. The central government has started to realize the importance of removing the policy burdens from state-owned enterprises through the two-decade reform, which was fully reflected in the 10th Five-Year Plan Outline[19] (*Outline*) approved by the 9th National People's Congress in 2001.

The *Outline* proposed a plan to remove the three aspects of the "social policy burdens". Firstly, the *Outline* proposed, in the foreword of the Chapter 18, "to basically establish a social security system of diversified capital resources, normalize the security system, and social-ize the administration service that is independent from enterprises and institutions in the 10th Five-Year Plan". In terms of the reform of state-owned enterprises, the key is to build the social security system that is independent from enterprises. In order to make up the historical debts in the social security funds, the *Outline* proposed in Sec. 2 of Chapter 18 to collect social security funds using several methods, including "to realize part of state-owned assets". Secondly, regarding state-owned enterprises' social functions in medical care, education, etc., the *Outline* suggested in Sec. 1 of Chapter 18 to "combine the overall social planning and

---

[19]*The Outline of the 10th Five-Year Plan for National Economic and Social Development of the People's Republic of China*, Xinhua Net.

individual accounts, carry out basic medical care insurance system for urban staff, and ensure staff's demands on basic medical care". Section 4 of Chapter 19 indicated to "strengthen the construction of community organizations and teams, expand the community's role in management, and carry out part of social and service functions that were removed from the enterprises and institutions as well as the governmental organizations". Thirdly, against the lay-off of surplus staff of state-owned enterprises, the *Outline* proposed to "gradually incorporate the basic living guarantee of laid-off staff of state-owned enterprises into the unemployment insurance based on pilots and expand the coverage of the unemployment insurance". At the same time, Sec. 1 of Chapter 18 of the *Outline* proposed to "develop labor-intensive industries of comparative advantages, develop the service enterprises, small- and medium-sized enterprises, and non-public enterprises that provide jobs, vigorously explore the international labor markets and increase the labor output". Beyond all doubts, the development of labor-intensive small- and medium-sized enterprises that meet the comparative advantages is the fundamental guarantee to maintain constant and rapid growth of the national economy and relieve the employment pressure.

According to the characteristics of state-owned enterprises and their products, four different strategies can be applied to solve the "strategic policy burden" of state-owned enterprises: (i) For the state-owned enterprises that are necessary for national defense and cannot be replaced, the government should support their production and development by financial appropriation, even though they are highly capital intensive and do not meet China's comparative advantages. Actually, there are only a few enterprises of this type. (ii) For capital-intensive, state-owned enterprises that manufacture domestic products, which occupy a large domestic market, they can establish joint ventures similar enterprises in developed countries or go public overseas to secure capital and technologies and overcome the comparative disadvantages of China. (iii) For capital-intensive state-owned enterprises that do not produce popular products in the domestic market, but own advantages in human capital, technologies, and experiences based on long-term accumulation, they can change the line of production to maximize favorable factors and minimize unfavorable factors and switch to labor-intensive products that occupy a large domestic market. (iv) For state-owned enterprises that do not have any edge in human capital and manufacture products that do not have any markets, they can only go bankrupt, merge, or restructure.

The *Outline* for the 10th Five-Year Plan also clarified the plan on the four reform strategies. In Sec. 2 of Chapter 16, *Outline* pointed out that "important enterprises that are vital to national security and economy should be held by the government". Section 1 of Chapter 16 also advocated that "the small number of enterprises under the monopolistic operation of the government can be transformed to wholly state-owned enterprises". Section 3 of Chapter 17 proposed to "encourage foreign capital especially the transnational companies to involve in the reorganization and transformation of state-owned enterprises, encourage qualified enterprises to issue stocks, and try to lower the financing cost". In Sec. 2 of Chapter 16, against the industrial structure of state-owned enterprises, the *Outline* proposed to "actively explore various effective ways, advancing or retreating, to facilitate the strategic adjustment of the layout of the national economy". For the policies on technologies, the Foreword of Chapter 4 of the *Outline* emphasized "to strengthen the transformation and upgrading of traditional industries and give full play to the comparative advantages in the labor-intensive industries". Regarding the structural adjustment of old industrial bases, the *Outline* proposed in Sec. 4 of Chapter 4 to "actively support and facilitate the transformation and structural adjustment of old industrial bases in Northeast China and some other places; give full play to their advantages in the solid foundation and talents; adjust the structure according to the layout of the state-owned economy; optimize the industrial structure, enterprise structure, and regional layout; form new competitive industries and enterprises; and establish new equipment manufacturing bases in qualified areas". Meanwhile, Sec. 3 of Chapter 4 advocated to "comprehensively apply economic, legal, and necessary administrative measures; shutdown factories and mines of low product quality that waste resources and cause serious pollution in unsafe production conditions; eliminate outmoded equipment and technologies; and compress the excessive and backward production capacity in some industries". For state-owned enterprises that suffered losses successively and can hardly be transformed, the *Outline* proposed, in Sec. 1 of Chapter 16, to "continue to implement the current policies for mergers and bankruptcy of state-owned enterprises, improve the market withdrawal mechanism, and apply bankruptcies for enterprises with a history of losses and with little hope of recovery according to laws".

The social and strategic policy burdens can be removed and the state-owned enterprises can possess the viability if the policies proposed in the *Outline* of the 10th Five-Year Plan are to be implemented. This would prompt managers of state-owned enterprises to be fully responsible for the performance of enterprises and the budget for these enterprises can be solidified. Based on this, a fair and competing market can be established for company governance, products, and managers, leading to the ultimate success of the reform of state-owned enterprises.

3.2. *Direction of the financial system reform*

The financial reform is undoubtedly the focus of China's current economic reform stage. As analyzed earlier, many problems in the financial system are actually derived from the problems of state-owned enterprises. The financial organizations are controlled by the government which also interferes in the financial system thus curtailing the reform of state-owned enterprises, which is, in fact, another form of "policy burden", for example, the soft budget constraint and the listing of state-owned enterprises in the stock market under the "quota system", etc. Similar to state-owned enterprises, these policy burdens would affect the performance and asset quality of financial organizations and meanwhile incur the moral hazard of managers of financial organizations. The problems of China's financial system cannot be fundamentally solved as long as the policy burdens of state-owned financial organizations and financial market remain unresolved.

In addition, for the long-term development of the financial system, special attention should be paid to the structural problems of the financial system. The demands of the real economy would promote the production and development of the financial system, so the development stages of the real economy and the characteristics of various financial arrangements should be considered to optimize the financial structure. At the starting stage of the economic development in China, the structure of comparatively rich labor and scarce capital would not be fundamentally changed in the short term, and the labor-intensive medium- and small-sized enterprises would become the most vigorous part of the economy. Therefore, the goal of the development of China's financial system, for a time, should be to establish a financial system with the medium- and small-sized financial organizations as the main body.

3.2.1. *Direction of the banking reform*

The non-performing loans of China's banking system are mainly incurred by the soft budget constraint of state-owned enterprises, but meanwhile, the large amount of non-performing assets are related to the moral hazard of the bank managers. Since the state-owned banks bear the policy burdens of state-owned enterprises, they would definitely suffer losses that result from these burdens. Owing to the information asymmetry, the government cannot tell whether the losses are due to the policy burdens or managers' poor operation, which would give rise to the problem of the moral hazard of bank managers, because the bank managers may impute the bad performance or losses of the banks to the policy burdens. Under these circumstances, the managers of state-owned banks often deviate from the operational goal of commercial banks, but would undertake efforts to complete government's orders. For example, the state-owned commercial banks had seen a rapid growth in loans in the first half of 2003, in stark contrast to the previous "credit grudging". Although it was a result of the economic improvement, the more direct reason was the government's order that required state-owned enterprises to lower the ratio of non-performing loans by 2% to 3% each year. However, it is, in fact, lowering the ratio of non-performing loans by blindly providing loans and can only offer temporary relief to the problem.

A great deal of discussions have taken place about the reform of state-owned commercial banks in China, including the reforms that are related to the internal operation and management system, such as the shareholding transformation and the improvement of the governance of banks; reforms to supplement the capital and lower the financial risks of banks, such as the listing of state-owned commercial banks; and the partition of state-owned commercial banks. Similar to the reform of state-owned enterprises, most reform measures currently focus on the reform of internal governance structure of banks, but, according to the same logic, the banking reform would only succeed when the policy burdens of the state-owned commercial banks are removed. Therefore, it is only possible to fundamentally solve the problem of the internal governance of banks after eliminating the policy burdens of the state-owned commercial banks to prevent them using these burdens as the excuse for the operational losses.

3.2.2. *Direction of the reform of the stock market*

Many problems in China's stock market are caused by the lack of "viability" in most listed companies. Many consider that the cause for the problems that constantly emerge in China's stock market is due to ineffective supervision. Although this is indeed the key point, the stock market can only be utilized as a tool to "collect money" if most listed companies lack viability, or their parent companies still have the social or strategic policy burdens. It is incorrect to believe that the stock market can be developed in a healthy way, only by strengthening the supervision.

A fundamental solution to the current problems in China's stock market is to remove the social and strategic policy burdens; reform the listed companies and their parent companies to enable them to obtain the viability that they can attain acceptable levels of profits based on routine nature of operations; and provide viability opportunities to privately held capital enterprises (in the three categories of Sino-joint venture, cooperative business, and exclusively foreign-owned enterprises in China) to be listed in China. Then, the supervision department can conduct truly effective supervision; the private investors and funds can win investment returns by holding stocks in the long run; and the overspeculations in the stock market can be improved. In this way, the stock market would positively contribute to the governance of listed companies, effective allocation of capitals, and the economic development of China.

3.2.3. *Establishment of the financial system with small- and medium-sized financial organizations as the main body*

At the starting stage of the economic development in China, the structure of comparatively rich labor and scarce capitals would not be fundamentally changed in the short term, and the labor-intensive medium- and small-sized enterprises would become the most vigorous part of the economy and play an important role in the growth of the national economy. However, the development of small- and medium-sized enterprises needs financial support, and they mainly rely on banks for external financing. Compared to the large banks, the small- and medium-sized banks hold more advantages in providing financial services to small- and medium-sized enterprises.[20] Therefore, China should vigorously develop small- and medium-sized financial organizations — especially the regional small- and medium-sized banks. The important goal in the construction of China's financial system is to build a financial system with small- and medium-sized financial organizations as the main body.

The establishment and reform of small- and medium-sized financial organizations have seen some positive changes in the recent years. For example, at the end of 2001, the People's Bank of China carried out a pilot project in rural financial reform in Jiangsu Province, when the rural commercial banks were set up in Zhangjiagang, Jiangyin, and Changshu, respectively. These rural commercial banks, originally credit cooperatives, had to completely let go of the organizational form of credit cooperatives and allowed people to hold the equity. Many farmers and private entrepreneurs competed to buy the shares. These rural commercial banks performed well in the recent two years after the establishment. However, several important problems should be noticed in the reform of small- and medium-sized banks. Firstly, no policy burden should be imposed on newly established small- and medium-sized financial organizations, otherwise the expected results of the reform cannot be reached. Secondly, the external supervision should be strengthened for the development of small- and medium-sized financial organizations because of the high operating risks. Without favorable external environment and supervision system, the managers may easily experience serious moral hazards. Finally, in addition to the external supervision, enough internal interests should be ensured, in order to issue licenses to small- and medium-sized financial organizations to hold a certain degree of monopoly, which would provide enough excitation to prevent them from experiencing moral hazards.

---

[20] See more details in Lin Yifu and Li Yongjun (2001). Development of small and medium financial organizations and financing of small and medium-sized enterprises. *Economic Research*. (1).

4. Conclusion

The reforms of state-owned enterprises and the financial system are undoubtedly the most important and core parts of the whole economic reform. Many problems in the Chinese economy are rooted in the problems of state-owned enterprises and the financial system. Between the two, the problem of state-owned enterprises is more fundamental, because many problems of the financial system are derived from the problems of state-owned enterprises.

The root of the problems of state-owned enterprises lies in their social and strategic policy burdens, as well as the problems of soft budget constraint and "viability" incurred from such a constraint. The previous reforms of state-owned enterprises were aimed at the internal governance structure of enterprises, such as the reforms of decentralization and interest concessions, contract system, and the modern enterprise system. However, the precondition for the successful reform of the internal governance structure of the enterprise is to relieve the information asymmetry, which requires the establishment of an effective external governance system as a precondition. In addition, the effective external governance mechanism cannot be built if the policy burdens of state-owned enterprises have not been removed, otherwise the information asymmetry cannot be relieved. Then the soft budget constraint and "viability" problems cannot be solved and the reform of state-owned enterprises would not fundamentally succeed. Therefore, the most profound problem of state-owned enterprises is the policy burden. The reform of the state-owned enterprises can only truly succeed if the policy burdens of state-owned enterprises are eliminated and the enterprises obtain viability.

The reform of the financial system is the focus and difficult point of the current stage of economic reform, but many problems in China's financial system are actually derived from problems in state-owned enterprises. Similar to the state-owned enterprises, Chinese financial organizations and the stock market also bear the policy burdens that promulgates they should provide capital at "lower prices" to state-owned enterprises and support the reform of state-owned enterprises. In addition, along with state-owned enterprises, the policy burdens would affect the performance and asset quality of financial organizations and bring about the moral hazards suffered by managers of financial organizations. The problems of China's financial system cannot be fundamentally solved if the policy burdens of the state-owned financial institutions and market are not eradicated.

At the same time, attention should be paid to the structural problems of the financial system for the long-term development of the financial system. The production and development of the financial system are promoted by the demands of the real economy, so the development stages of the real economy and the characteristics of various financial arrangements should be considered to optimize the financial structure. For the starting stage of the Chinese economy, the structure of comparatively rich labor and scarce capitals would not be fundamentally changed in the short term, and the labor-intensive medium- and small-sized enterprises would necessarily become the most vigorous part of the economy and make important contributions to the economic growth. Compared to large financial institutions and financial market, the small- and medium-sized financial institutions hold more advantages in providing financial services to small- and medium-sized enterprises. Therefore, the goal of the development of China's financial system, for a time, should be to establish a financial system with the medium- and small-sized financial institutions as the main body.

Chapter 10

The Development Pattern of the Chinese Financial Market in the New Century* — Forward: China's Tasks in the New Century

For more than two decades, China's comprehensive national force, social productivity, people's living standards, and international status have attained an unprecedented improvement through reform and opening up. The People's Republic of China has ushered in 21st century with a brand-new look. However, China is still a developing country with comparatively low per-capita income. In the new century, China faces the task of sustaining the pace of its economic development. The rural population in China accounts for approximately 70% of the total population and the per-capita incomes of the rural population are even lower than half of the per-capita incomes of the urban population, so the income gap between the urban and rural areas should be narrowed further. In order to participate in the ongoing economic globalization, China is putting forth great efforts on her accession into the World Trade Organization (WTO). Adjustments shall be made to production, trade, and employment structures to enable the Chinese economy to withstand severe tests in every aspect.

In the new century, reforms shall be intensified to maintain a healthy and sustainable development of the economy. The reform of the economic system has made remarkable achievements in over the 20 years period,

*This chapter is the summary of the topic of the presentation made in the Chinese Economy 50 Forum on December 24, 2000. The author thanks Liu Peilin for helping in sorting out the first draft of this chapter.

except the lagging reforms in the financial system. The financial system involves every aspect of social and economic life. It is more difficult to reform the financial system compared to other aspects of the economic system. However, the financial system is the source of various conflicts in the economy, so many of the economy's profound problems cannot be solved, and therefore, constant economic growth cannot be guaranteed without the proper reform of the financial system. The next steps in the reform of the financial system become a key link to the whole strategic layout of the reform, which has attracted global attention. A consensus has not been reached on the direction of reforms and the development pattern of the financial system. Some advocate imitating the developed countries in order to develop a financial system mainly relying on super large banks, the main-board stock market, and growth enterprise securities market (GEM). However, this idea may not work as international financial systems vary among developed countries. It is also necessary to analyze whether the practices of developed countries can be followed in China. In parallel, the basic functions and characteristics of such financial systems must be studied to derive a logic for the creation of an effective Chinese financial system.

1. Criteria for the Efficiency of Different Financial Market Systems and the Evolution Laws

1.1. *Functions of the financial market and the criteria for the efficiency of the financial market*

The financial market essentially depends on and serves the development of the real economy. Households, companies, and governmental organizations expect sustainable income and expense flow in the real economy. Owing to the uncharacteristic income and expense flow in various economies, some economies may have capital surpluses, while others may be in shortage of capital. Most financial requirements of an economy rely on the financial market. The basic function of the financial market is to make an accommodation between capital supply and its demand by different economies, by mobilizing the capital from enterprises that enjoy capital surpluses and allocating them to those that need it based on certain criteria.

In the two functions of the financial market, the allocation of capital is more fundamental, because under given conditions, higher efficiency of capital allocation would generate more economic surplus and guarantee more capital for mobilization. In addition, based on higher efficiency of capital allocation, the return rate of capital would be higher; people would be more willing to deposit money; the more economic surplus would be utilized in savings/investments, the more capital would be mobilized. Therefore, the fundamental criterion to judge the efficiency of the financial market is whether the capital can be allocated to industrial departments and enterprises of the highest return rate in order to enhance the rapid development of the real economy. If the capital can be constantly allocated to the industrial departments and enterprises of the highest return rate, then the growth of the national economy and the capitals mobilized from households, companies, and governmental organizations would be maximized.

1.2. *Evolution laws of the financial market model*

In the process of economic development, continuous changes have occurred in the financial system. On the one hand, new organizations in the financial market along with new financial instruments have been constantly created, such as banks, stock markets, and various financial assets. Generally speaking, the financial market consists of two basic financing methods: (i) direct financing, represented by banks and (ii) indirect financing, represented by the stock markets. Each of the two methods has its own advantages and disadvantages,[1] so it is difficult to tell which is better for capital owners and which is better for capital users. On the other hand, the comparative structure of financing has been constantly changing in different development stages of different financial market organizations, thus revealing the requirements of the economy. In different development stages, the most active industrial sectors of the economy give full play to their own comparative advantages, and thus reap the greatest profitability.

---

[1]From the perspective of the capital users, the cost of bank financing is lower than the financing of the stock market, but the risk is bigger. For the capital owners, the estimated capital returns from the investment in the stock market are higher than the deposit in banks, despite the bigger risks.

Therefore, the inherent laws for the evolution of the financial market must comply with the demands emerging from developing a real economy and constantly allocate capital to such production industries that are most accordant with the comparative advantages in the specific development stage. It is a dynamic criterion to measure the efficiency of the financial market.

In this aspect, it is not wise to hold a preconceived view that one organization of the financial market is better than the other, or a particular financial organization structure is better than the other. The selection of the mode of the financial system should be based on whether it can comply with the demands of the competitive industries in the real economy. By predicting the profitable industrial sectors for the future, China would be able to build a roadmap for its financial market.

2. China's Advantageous Industries in the Early 21st Century

A popular, yet inaccurate, idea in domestic theoretical circles and executive departments is that under the fierce global economic competition China would be strong enough to compete internationally by developing capital-intensive enterprises or top technologies. However, the reality is that China is still in the catching-up phase. Actually, the competitiveness of industries relies on the cost of the production. Lower costs can strengthen the competitiveness factor. The level of costs in a certain period is mainly decided by whether the industry has given full play to the comparative advantages in a country or a region in that period.

The comparative advantage is conditioned by the factor endowment structure of a country or a region. Currently, the factor endowment structure in China is featured with relatively scarce capital and abundant labor supply, so it should focus on the labor-intensive production that complies with the comparative advantages. These productive activities include lower technological levels in high-technology industries, such as the hardware assembly in the information technology (IT) industry, as well as other corresponding sections in labor-intensive industries. The productive activities within these industrial sections are competitive and are capable of self-development.

On the contrary, productive activities that are outside such industrial sections have no "viability" in the market competition and cannot accumulate and develop by themselves. Under China's current factor endowment structure, a new round of catching-up strategy, regardless of the existing conditions of the country, needs to be launched in order to carry out productive activities that are without the viability. The catching-up strategy refers to lowering the capital prices and adopting the policy protections for numerous trades and industries. Although such productive activities, without the viability, can be set up based on the protection under the current factor endowment structure, they are not competitive in the market and are low in the capital return rate. As a result, the objects that are supported by the catching-up strategy cannot accumulate capital. It would restrict productive activities with viability from obtaining resources, limit their activities, and significantly reduce capital accumulation overall. Owing to the two aspects, it would finally lower the rate of capital accumulation below acceptable levels, leading to fewer and fewer capital mobilization by the government to support the productive activities without viability. The whole financial market cannot be rationalized. The new round of catching-up strategy may fail and affect the entire economy adversely. If the country complies to market forces and vigorously develops the productive activities with viability, then the economic surplus of each production period can be maximized, the social capital reserves and per-capita amount of the capital held would grow at the highest speed, leading to an abundant supply of capital, compared to the scarce labor. Under the factor endowment structure at this development stage, enterprises with viability that accord to China's comparative advantages would naturally become more capital intensive with advanced technologies, laying the solid foundation for an advanced industrial structure. Therefore, it seems that the development of labor-intensive industrial sections of comparative advantages is not as effective as the catching-up strategy in improving the industrial structure in the short term. However, in the long run, the strategy of the comparative advantage is the only correct road for the sustainable development of the economy.

Therefore, by early 21st century, the most competitive enterprises in China are those with viability, with small- and medium-sized enterprises as the main body. The direction of reforms in China's financial market is to ensure that the financing demands of these enterprises are met.

3. Selection of China's Financial Market Model

Labor-intensive medium- and small-sized enterprises would be the most active business forms in China's industrial structure for a long time to come. Although China has established the central bank system, started the commercialization of banks, and set up securities and insurance market through the 20-year reform, the current financial system that relies mainly on the four major state-owned commercial banks and supplemented by the stock market cannot well serve the labor-intensive small- and medium-sized enterprises.

Compared to small- and medium-sized banks, large banks can hardly provide financial service for small- and medium-sized enterprises.

Large banks cannot provide sound financial services to small- and medium-sized enterprises. Firstly, the transaction cost per unit of fund is comparatively high for financial services provided by large banks to small- and medium-sized enterprises. With higher capital requirements, the large banks would set more approval links and long approval chains for the issuance of loans. If a sum of capital is granted to a large project as a loan, the complicated approval procedures should be completed only once, so the transaction cost per unit of fund would be comparatively low. However, if this sum of capital is distributed to several small- and medium-sized projects, the complicated approval procedures would be completed several times, leading to a comparatively higher transaction cost. From the perspective of small- and medium-sized enterprises, it is more economical to apply for loans from the small- and medium-sized banks than the large banks for the same amount, since the approval procedure of the small- and medium-sized banks is simpler.

Secondly, the information cost is comparatively high for financial services provided by large banks to small- and medium-sized enterprises. Banks need to thoroughly examine the credit worthiness of enterprises applying for loans and monitor the use of such loans after issuance, which significantly rely on the information about the quality of the enterprise's projects and their management levels. Large banks have to adopt a multilevel branch agent system owing to their large scale, which suffers from frequent personnel turnover. The staff members of banks may be promoted, demoted, or transferred according to their performance, so the banks' personnel find it cumbersome to accumulate sufficient information on the small-

and medium-sized enterprises of a region. Even if the staff members of local branches understand the operation status of local small- and medium-sized enterprises, they are inefficient in delivering such information to a higher level. The operation information of small- and medium-sized enterprises is not as transparent as listed companies, owing to the lack of restriction in the information disclosure system. Lack of transparency in collecting information about small- and medium-sized enterprises makes it difficult for the bank managers to explain any loan-related problems to the higher level. Large banks can accumulate the information more easily for large enterprises and large projects. Distinguished from large banks, small- and medium-sized banks mainly serve enterprises within a comparatively smaller region. The small-sized banks know a great deal about the operation, management, and credit of numerous small- and medium-sized enterprises in their regions and can accumulate information more easily. Therefore, the information cost on large banks, that provide loans to small- and medium-sized enterprises, is higher than the small- and medium-sized banks.

Thirdly, large banks have more opportunities owing to their abundant funds and often ignore the loans to small- and medium-sized enterprises, so it is difficult for them to establish a stable and close cooperative relationship with small- and medium-sized enterprises or solve the information asymmetry problem between financial institutions and small- and medium-sized enterprises. Therefore, large financial institutions pay less attention to the provision of loans to small- and medium-sized enterprises.

4. The Main-Board Securities Market Cannot be the Financing Source for Small- and Medium-Sized Enterprises Owing to the High Cost of Financing

The securities market includes both the stock and enterprise bonds market. As is known to all, a high threshold is set up to access financing in stock and enterprise bonds market. Enterprises in the market should qualify the requirements on capital, turnover, and amount of profits. Therefore, only a few enterprises are qualified even in the developed countries such as America, and only more than 7,000 companies are listed in the New York stock market. A large number of small- and medium-sized enterprises are unqualified to be listed for stock and bond financing. On the other hand, enterprises applying for listing employ professional accounting and auditing service organizations to conduct professional assessment for listing, and the service costs millions of U.S. dollars in foreign countries and also costs much in China. It is not economical for small- and medium-sized enterprises that need only a small amount of capital to pay the high cost. Meanwhile, listed companies are mostly of limited liability and are required by the supervisory authorities to disclose information about their operations in every fixed or indefinite period to protect the interests of the investors. In order to ensure fairness, correctness, and legitimacy of the disclosed information, independent professional accounting and auditing service organizations are often involved, which also leads to high cost. From the perspective of small- and medium-sized enterprises, it is not economical for them to obtain funds from the stock and enterprise bond market.

5. The Growth Enterprise Securities Market (GEM) is not Suitable for Chinese Small- and Medium-Sized Enterprises

As the Chinese financial system mainly relying on large banks and supplemented by the stock market cannot well serve the most active small- and medium-sized enterprises, the financing demands of small- and medium-sized enterprises are met through the GEM. However, owing to its special service objective, GEM too cannot service the labor-intensive small- and medium-sized enterprises.

Firstly, the GEM can never be the main source for the initial funding required by small- and medium-sized enterprises. If a limited liability company can be registered and listed on the GEM based only on their "creativity", the problems of adverse selection and moral hazard would necessarily prevail in the GEM, which may finally lead to the collapse of market.

Secondly, in developed countries, GEM provides capital for risky ventures. Such capital may be used in research, development, and trial production of enterprises with human capital. GEM also provides withdrawal channel for risk capital and capital to enterprises to expand their markets.

Thirdly, despite the lower threshold for listing in GEM, rather than the main-board market, its listing assessment fee is expensive. According to statistics, the fees on the financing of National Association of Securities Dealers Automated Quotations (NASDAQ) account for 13% to 18%, no less than US$300,000 to US$500,000. However, the stock profits fluctuate violently owing to the risks of high technologies and market of the enterprises in GEM. Because of the limited liability system and the separation of the ownership and management, the cost for financing in GEM is certainly higher than the cost for bank loans, and even higher than the cost for financing in the main-board market.

GEM first arose in the America. Until now, the only mature GEM of the world was the American NASDAQ where two factors affecting the real economy can be found: (i) America's per-capita capital occupies among the front ranks of the whole world and (ii) America, at the forefront of the world technologies, has to maintain its technological progress and economic growth through a great deal of research and development (R&D) activities. While fewer R&D activities are conducted by large enterprises or governmental organizations, a majority of such activities in emerging technologies are conducted by many small- and medium-sized enterprises. These R&D activities carry high risks. If the enterprises had considered development trends in the market during their R&D activities, they are bound to experience rapid growth and investors would earn large returns. However, it is believed that most enterprises would fail in R&D or can hardly occupy the market with the developed products, with only one or two enterprises surviving finally. Enterprises suffer the risk of operational failure and capital investors may sustain huge losses, so the banks rarely provide capital to these enterprises. On the other hand, owing to America's high per-capita capital level, the return rate would be low when large amount of capital is invested in traditional production technologies according to the law of diminishing returns. More capital should be invested into projects of higher estimated return rate, which gives rise to risk investment and NASDAQ.

Labor-intensive small- and medium-sized enterprises are the most active forms of enterprises in China. However, they differ from the small- and medium-sized enterprises of advanced technology and market risks in the GEM of America in that the Chinese enterprises are featured with low cost, low risk, and rapid imitation and introduction of technologies. They are free from the risks associated with advanced technology and markets as they own stable product market and mature technologies. Therefore, the operation and management level is the main risk for labor-intensive small- and medium-sized enterprises, but GEM obviously can do nothing about this risk. In addition, as reported by the *Liberation Daily* on September 16, 2000, the proposed listing threshold for GEM is tangible assets of 8 million yuan, registered capital of 10 million yuan, and increase of sales income of the primary business by 30%. If the threshold for China's GEM is confirmed as such, the labor-intensive small- and medium-sized enterprises of mature technologies, with stable market prospects and listing can secure loans from banks, and do not need to finance in the GEM with such a high cost.

6. How to Regard the Merger Wave of Foreign Banking Industries and Large Banks' Expansion to Personal Credit?

There is currently an international wave of merger of banking industries and the large banks' expansion to serve personal credit in the developed countries. Therefore, quite a few Chinese scholars oppose the development of small- and medium-sized banks and advocate strengthening the merger of banks and expanding the scale of banks to compete with foreign large banks. However, any innovation in the financial field is generated based only on the requirements of the economy. The merger of foreign large banks results from the expansion of transnational corporations, business scale, production layout, and capital demands. Large banks' expansion to serve personal credit in developed countries is based on their advanced recording system on the personal credit status, while China and many emerging industrialized countries do not share this base. In addition, large banks in developed countries mainly issue consumer credit to individuals. Compared to the loans for operations and fixed capital, the consumer credit enjoys better material mortgage with better loan quality and is easier to supervise.

7. Conclusion

Labor-intensive small- and medium-sized enterprises can mostly give full play to China's comparative advantage in the factor endowment structure. To facilitate the economic development of China, the best method is to vigorously develop the labor-intensive small- and medium-sized enterprises that will solve the unemployment pressure, narrow the income gap between the urban and rural areas, and effectively manage the challenges after entry into the WTO. The small- and medium-sized banks are required to solve the financing problems of labor-intensive small- and medium-sized enterprises. The solution lies in China developing small- and medium-sized banks to service this segment. Of course, China, as a large country, needs to carry out some large projects as well as some enterprises are large enough to finance in the stock market.

However, some small- and medium-sized financial institutions in China suffer more bad debts than the large banks, so quite a few researchers doubt the development of small- and medium-sized banks. In fact, this is the result of insufficient attention to the small- and medium-sized financial institutions in the past. China has often inhibited the development of small- and medium-sized banks for a long time to prevent them struggling against large banks for capital. Along with economic development, the demands on small- and medium-sized banks have increased. The government started to relax their policies and indulged the development of small- and medium-sized financial institutions, leading to the lack of supervision. As a special product, financing meets the problem of information asymmetry in the transaction, so the problem of moral hazard would become very serious without good supervision. Since China inhibited the development of small- and medium-sized banks and did not apply a proper supervision system when the development was permitted, many problems emerged. If, again, the development is inhibited to prevent these problems, the financial system that contributes to China's economic development cannot be established. As the new century is unfolding, China should continue efforts in developing small- and medium-sized banks, supplemented by large banks and the stock market. For the development of small- and medium-sized banks, the government should (i) lower the threshold, (ii) release the restrictions on the access, and (iii) strengthen the supervision.

Chapter 11

On the Optimal Financial Structure in Economic Development

1. The Economic Development Stage and Characteristics of the Financial Structure

The history of economic development in developed countries reveals that the financial systems varied in different development stages. In addition, developing and developed countries differ from each other in the financial structure. Different financial systems in different development stages indicate that the structure of the financial system is related to the development stages in some way.

Although the same economy has different structures of the financial system in different development stages, the financial systems share common basic functions, mainly to mobilize capital allocate capitals, and spread risks. The most fundamental among these functions is the effective allocation of capital. Only based on the effective allocation of capital, the capital available in each period can be allocated to the best-performing enterprises in the most competitive industry to produce maximum social surplus, highest capital return rate, maximum proportion of the newly created social surplus utilized in accumulation (instead of consumption). Therefore, the ability to mobilize capital depends on the effectiveness of capital allocation. In the same way, risks can only be minimized when capital is allocated to the best-performing enterprises in the most competitive industry, so the ability of the diversification of risk also relies on the function of allocation.

Owing to different characteristics of industries and enterprises of greatest competitiveness and highest investment return rate, the optimum financial structure in different development stages would change with changes in the characteristics of the industries and enterprises in different development stages.[1] This is because the financial systems share the same basic functions where the efficiency of the financial system depends on capital allocation. If the financial structure at a certain development stage deviates from the optimum structure determined by the characteristics of the real economy, the economic development would be adversely affected. If the development of real economy and the evolution of the financial structure show a dynamic and positive interaction, the economy would develop successfully — otherwise obstructions, or even crises, may occur. To be more specific, the optimum financial structure of an economy in a certain development stage is decided by the interaction between the characteristics of various financial arrangements and the characteristics of industries and enterprises of the real economy. On the one hand, an economy owns different structures of factor endowment in different development stages. At the early stages of economic development, capital is scarce and labor is comparatively abundant, but at the later stages of economic development, capital is comparatively abundant and labor becomes comparatively scarce.[2] The change of the relative availability degree of capital and labor in the factor endowment structure determines the differences in the industrial and technological structures of the real economy, as enterprises in different industries and industrial sections have different risk characteristics and the scale of fund demands in their productive activities. On the other hand, financial activities are commonly featured with incompatible excitation, information asymmetry, and very unequal responsibilities. Different financial arrangements show their own advantages and disadvantages in overcoming the above problems and require different transaction costs for financing. Therefore, in order to

---

[1] Of course, despite being in the same development stage, different countries reveal diversified characteristics in the financial structures owing to the effect of the legal environment and path dependence, such as the British and American systems that are featured with direct stock financing and the Japanese and German systems that are featured with the indirect bank financing. However, other factors show less impact than the characteristics of the real economy. The financial structures of Britain, America, Japan and Germany, were all featured with regional small- and medium-sized banks and informal financial institutions at the early stages of economic development.

[2] The natural resources are also incorporated in the factor endowment structure. To simplify the discussion, we assume that only capital and labor are incorporated. The same conclusion would be reached after the natural resources are included, but the discussion would be more complicated.

realize the rational distribution of financial resources, the optimum financial structure should guarantee that the institutional arrangements in the financial system and their internal relations would confer with the scale of industries, technologies, and enterprise structures and the risk characteristics.

2. Brief Overview of the Structure of Real Economy and Risk Characteristics

The most competitive industry, product, and technology structure of a country is decided by the factor endowment structure. Therefore, in order to minimize the production cost, the selection of the industry, product, and technology should be based upon the characteristics of the relative prices of corresponding factors in the fair and competitive market economy, where the relative prices of factors are decided by the relative availability of capital and labor in the factor endowment structure of the country. In an open and competitive market, an economy with comparatively scarce capital and abundant supply of labor would lead to comparatively high capital and low labor prices. Faced with these relative prices of factors, enterprises should select labor-intensive enterprises within the comparatively capital-intensive industries, and produce products with labor-intensive technologies, in order to obtain their own viability. On the contrary, in an economy of comparatively rich capital and scarce labor, enterprises should select relatively capital-intensive products with comparatively capital-intensive technologies, based on their consideration of the viability. In the open and competitive market, since the selection of industry, product, and technology structure is decided by the relative availability of capital and labor in the factor endowment structure, any upgrading of capital in this structure would be fundamentally determined by the upgrading of the capital in the factor endowment structure. Enterprises in different industries that produce different products with different technologies encounter different risk characteristics and requirements of funds.

An enterprise may face two types of risks: (i) the innovation risk for products and technologies and (ii) the entrepreneur risk (including the operation capacity risk and moral risk).[3]

---

[3]Risks incurred by the market fluctuation are not considered here.

Innovation risks refer to enterprises' risks in introducing newer products and technologies in their industries. An enterprise in a developing may be developing products and technologies that may be more labor intensive when compared to a similar enterprise with greater comparative advantages in a developed economy. Such enterprises in the developing economy would benefit by upgrading their existing technologies and products and introducing newer technologies from developed countries. Then the innovation risks for technologies and products of this enterprise are lower. On the contrary, if no other enterprise in the same or another economy holds more comparative advantage, then the enterprise would need to input a large amount of manpower and materials on research and development (R&D) in order to innovate its technologies and products. R&D activities are very risky. Even if the R&D activities succeed, it is still uncertain whether the enterprise can obtain the patent for the new technology and product and how would they be accepted by the consumers. Innovation is therefore considered very risky. However, if the R&D activities have succeeded and the new products are accepted by the market and are protected by the patents, the enterprise may occupy the whole market and enjoy monopoly profits. On the contrary, if an enterprise succeeds in innovation, other similar enterprises may also introduce the same technologies, so the competition would be very fierce, where each enterprise can only take up a part of the market share.

The entrepreneurial risk is led by the different capital owners and capital users. Firstly, the entrepreneurs' judgment on the selection of technologies, products, and industries and the operation and management ability would affect the profitability of enterprises and further influence the enterprises' ability in repayment of debts or in the distribution of dividends to investors. Secondly, owing to the incompatible excitation, information asymmetry, and unequal responsibilities, the enterprises may not pay off their debts or the operators may occupy the assets and incomes belonging to investors.

Developing countries have comparatively scarce capital and abundant labor. Therefore, developing countries hold comparative advantages in labor-intensive industries and labor-intensive sections in the capital-intensive industries. Such enterprises require comparatively smaller scales of capital investment, with most of them as the small- and medium-sized enterprises. Based on an analysis about the world economic development levels, all industries where developing countries hold the comparative advantages benefit from mature products and technologies, and most enterprises can realize these technologies and products by introduction or imitation. Therefore, enterprises in developing countries share low innovation risks on technologies and products, but their main risks come from the operational ability and moral hazards. The optimum financial structure in developing countries should effectively overcome the entrepreneur risks, provide financial services to small- and medium-sized enterprises with lower transaction costs, and thus allocate the limited financial resources to industries and enterprises of comparative advantages.

The economies of developed countries are all featured with relatively abundant capital and relatively scarce labor in their resource endowment structure. Therefore, barring the relatively labor-intensive small- and medium-sized enterprises providing non-tradable commodities and services that satisfy the local living needs, other enterprises that provide tradable commodities and services are can emerge as leaders only when they invest in independent R&D on new products and technologies. These enterprises are faced with the problems of operational ability, moral risks of entrepreneurs and huge innovation risks for technologies and products. At the same time, they require large-scale capital financing. It is expected that the financial systems of developed countries would support such enterprises and scale of their capital demands.

3. On the Nature and Application of Various Arrangements of Financial Systems

The financial structure of a country can be viewed from several perspectives. The method of financing, i.e., direct and indirect is determined by whether financial intermediaries are needed in the financial activities; the financial system can be divided into the money market and capital market according to the terms of the financial transaction; and the formal and informal financing can be determined according to whether the financial activities are supervised by the central financial authority, etc. This chapter mainly views the financial structure from the first aspect (see Table 11.1).

The direct financing method mainly refers to the direct transaction between both parties in the financial market, or the direct transaction through the intermediary institutions, which is generally completed by

Table 11.1. Comparison of the Characteristics of Financial Arrangements.

	Direct stock financing		Indirect bank financing	
Capital supplier	High return	High risk	Low return	Low risk
Enterprises in need of capitals	High cost	Low risk	Low cost	High risk

the issuance and transaction of stocks.[4] In direct financing, the capital supplier can earn dividends only if the enterprise makes profits, but would enjoy no return if the enterprise does not make profits. For liquidation of enterprises on account of bankruptancy, only when there are surpluses after the repayment of the enterprises' liabilities, the stock investors would receive a part of the surplus according to the proportion of their investment amount. Indirect financing mainly refers to capital financing with banks as the intermediaries, i.e., the capital suppliers deposit their capital in banks, and then banks provide such capital to different enterprises as loans, to realize the mobilization and allocation of social surplus. In indirect financing, commercial banks take nearly all investment risks, while the capital suppliers assume smaller risks. Except when the banks go bankrupt owing to the bank runs, banks would repay the principal and interest to capital suppliers on time. Therefore, compared to the bank intermediaries, the direct financing shows bigger risks for capital owners, so generally, enterprises have to provide higher estimated returns than banks' interests to capital suppliers, in order to make up the high risks and absorb capital suppliers to invest on enterprises' stocks. For capital suppliers, direct financing is featured with high risks, but high estimated returns, while the indirect financing is low in both risks and returns. Therefore, it is impossible to decide which financial arrangement is better based only on the characteristics of direct and indirect financing since both of them have their own advantages and disadvantages.

Secondly, for the direct financing in the stock market, irrespective of whether enterprises earn profits or not, and whether they distribute dividends or not, they should repay the principal and interest on time. If the enterprises fail to repay the principal and interest on time, banks can force

---

[4]Direct financing also includes enterprise bonds, whose characteristics are placed between the stock and bank loans. In order to simplify the discussion, it is not discussed here.

to conduct bankruptcy liquidation on enterprises, when the stock investors or the shareholders, cannot ask the enterprise to return the equity capital unless all shareholders refuse the enterprise bankruptcy. Therefore, from the perspective of enterprises, indirect bank financing is riskier than direct financing from the stock market. However, the interest for the bank loan is generally lower than the dividends distributed to the stock shareholders, so the cost of indirect bank financing is lower than direct financing from the stock market. Direct financing is featured with low risks, but higher costs, while indirect financing is featured with high risks but low costs, so it is difficult to say which financial arrangement is better based only on their characteristics.[5]

For single capital suppliers, especially the suppliers of a small amount of capital, detailed information and high supervision cost are required in supervising the enterprises in need of capital. Although the financial supervision authorities in various countries would require the stock issuers to reveal some information, the information asymmetry between both sides of the capital supply and demand is still very serious. In addition, enterprises distribute dividends only when they make money. When enterprises enter bankruptcy, indirect financing can earn interests on time, but the direct capital suppliers face greater investment risks. In direct financing, an institutional arrangement to overcome or relieve the problem of information asymmetry is to conduct circulation transaction in the secondary market with direct financing tools, such as stocks and securities. For example, small shareholders "vote with their feet" and utilize the ups and downs of relevant stock prices in order to promote the managers of joint-stock companies to care more about the interests of shareholders. In addition, single capital suppliers can spread investment risks by selecting rational investment portfolios. Owing to weak supervision by the capital suppliers, direct financing may be preferred. In addition, in stock financing, enterprises

---

[5] For capital suppliers, the enterprise bonds are featured with higher risks than bank deposits, but lower risks than the stock investment, while the returns are also between the stocks and bank deposits. For enterprises, the enterprise bonds enjoy lower costs than bank loans, but only enterprises with a high reputation are qualified to issue the enterprise bonds. In addition, the enterprises are required to reveal information and satisfy the requirements of the financial authorities, thus leading to higher transaction costs. Therefore, we cannot ascertain whether this financial arrangement is better than the others based only on the characteristics of the enterprise bonds.

distributed dividends only when they make money. If enterprises fail, they do not repay the funds and so bear the least risks. However, owing to information asymmetry, enterprises should disclose relevant information to persuade capital suppliers to purchase the stocks or bonds of the enterprises and pay more remuneration to investors. Therefore, the cost of direct financing is very high.

Indirect financing mainly refers to the capital financing through the banks as the intermediaries. The capital suppliers deposit capital in the banks and then banks concentrate such capital and provide them to different enterprises as loans to realize mobilization and allocation of social surplus. In indirect financing, commercial banks take nearly all investment risks, while the capital suppliers assume least risks, except when the banks go bankrupt owing to the bank runs. Banks are required to repay principal and interest to capital suppliers. Capital suppliers would thus obtain lower investment return rate than they would secure under direct financing. Commercial banks have their own mechanism to lower the investment risks. For example, firstly, they operate under the supervision of the central financial supervision authority, with the deposit reinsurance mechanism; secondly, as professional intermediaries, commercial banks can give full play to their scale advantages in obtaining information about capital debtors, prior selection of debtors and subsequent supervision, and lower the information cost; and thirdly, such banks with great amount of capital can spread the investment risks by selection of investment portfolios. The borrowers of indirect financing have to go through strict selection procedures and supervision of banks in their applications for the use of and repayment of loans, but borrowers do not need to disclose their enterprises information and only need to directly transact with one or several banks, so the financing cost would be significantly decreased owing to the low transaction cost.

In indirect financing, the industrial organization structure of the banking industry is a very important aspect of the financial structure, especially the ratio of nationwide large banks to regional small- and medium-sized banks. Owing to the small scale of capital, regional small- and medium-sized banks enjoy advantages in collecting and accumulating information about local small- and medium-sized enterprises, instead of providing loans to large enterprises. Therefore, these regional small- and medium-sized banks are required to provide financial services to small- and medium-sized enterprises in need of a small amount of capital. On the contrary, large nationwide banks can mobilize and allocate capital in a wider range and are capable of providing financial services to large enterprises in need of a large amount of capital. At the same time, large banks are generally not willing to provide financial services to small- and medium-sized enterprises because it is difficult for them to obtain relevant information about small- and medium-sized enterprises and the information and transaction costs per unit of loans are relatively high, owing to the small scale of capital required by small- and medium-sized enterprises.

The financial transaction methods mentioned earlier belong to formal financing. Various informal financing methods hold their own unique advantages in providing financial service at a smaller scale owing to the flexible transaction methods and low information costs.

4. Evolution of the Financial Structure: Dynamic Matching of the Arrangements of Financial Systems and the Structure of the Real Economy

As mentioned earlier, the optimum financial structure of an economy in a development stage is determined by the characteristics of the risks and financial activities, as well as the nature of various arrangements of the financial systems. The optimum financial structure at each development stage should match the various arrangements of financial systems and internal relations to the industrial, product, and technological structures of the real economy and the characteristics of the enterprises, in order to spread the risks effectively and optimize the allocation of resources. Along with the upgrading of resources endowment structure and the change of the industrial and technological structures of the real economy, the optimum financial structure of an economy would change accordingly.

Although there are many small- and medium-sized enterprises in developed countries, the large enterprises and R&D enterprises that require a large amount of capitals dominate the national economy. These enterprises encounter the operation ability and moral risks of entrepreneurs and even more risks in market and technologies. Therefore, in addition to large banks providing short-term and large-amount of finance to large enterprises, an effective financial system should also incorporate direct financing of the stock market that can effectively spread the risks in the market related to new products and technologies. The stock market consists of the main-board market with a successful operational history and products occupying large market shares, which serve the large companies, as well as the risk investment and GEM that provide financial services to the innovation-oriented small- and medium-sized enterprises of high potential growth and risks. A bond market should also be set up to meet the financial requirements of reputable large enterprises with good reputation. Of course, small- and medium-sized financial institutions should also be established to serve the labor-intensive small- and medium-sized enterprises.

A trade-off between the risks and returns (costs) exists in every financial arrangement. Therefore, the optimum financial structure can also be confirmed by matching the real economy's characteristics and the financial arrangements' characteristics, instead of the financial arrangements themselves.

Regardless of the problems, such as the speculation and economic bubbles, the risk of the whole society would be lower if the real financial structure is able to follow the theoretically optimum financial structure, while the risk would be greater if there is a discord between theory and practice.

In developing countries, labor-intensive industries hold comparative advantages, where enterprises are generally small in scale and require huge capital and suffer entrepreneur risks. Therefore, indirect financing with regional small- and medium-sized banks as the main body, should be regarded as the basis of the financial system in the developing countries. Of course, direct financing of large banks and the securities market has its place in a developing economy owing to the presence of few large enterprises. However, if developing countries blindly imitate the financial structure of developed countries regardless of the state of their economic development, it would distort the resource allocation, lower the service efficiency of resources,[6] and slow down or even inhibit the development pace.

---

[6]The situation is happening in many developing countries.

Chapter 12

Lack of Existing Paradigm for Interpreting the Chinese Economy*

1. How to View the Previous 25 Years of Rapid Economic Growth?

Understanding China's past is the basis for understanding its future because it is the past historical events that help shaping the present China. Since China's history is lengthy and extensive, only the previous 30 years will be discussed here.

The following story is the author's personal experience:

In 1987, I returned to Beijing from America, where I had just earned my doctorate degree in economics. At that time, I was the first to return to China after receiving a doctorate in social science from either Europe or America. The government released a special policy during this time to encourage students who were studying abroad to return to China for work, mainly because they could bring a car back to China that was free from duty tax. The tariff on cars was as high as 215%. I brought back a car and registered it at the Beijing Traffic Control Department, where I was told that my car was the second registered private car in all of Beijing. In contrast, the family cars in Beijing reached 2 million, including more than 1 million private cars, by 2002.

The past 25 years have been very prosperous for China. Initially, China set a goal of quadrupling the economy in 20 years, with an annual growth of 7%, but few people in the world believed that China could achieve this goal. At that time, more than 80% of the Chinese population was living in rural areas, and most of them were illiterate. It was the first time in history that such a big agricultural country with such a low development

---

*This chapter was published in the *Economic Daily* on December 8, 2003.

level could maintain its development with an annual growth rate of 7% for more than 20 years. In the 25 years between 1978 and 2002, the average annual economic growth rate had reached 9.3% and the Chinese economy had increased 8.5 times. The growth rate and the current scale have far exceeded the goal that was proposed in 1978.

The indicator to measure the economic openness of a country's economy is simply the country's dependence on foreign trade, i.e., the proportion of the total import and export in gross domestic product (GDP). In 1978, China's dependence on foreign trade amounted to only 9.5%. However, Chinese foreign trade has increased 30 times in the past 25 years, and the dependence on foreign trade grew 50% in 2002. Both the figures have never been achieved before by another economic power. As regards trade power, Japan's dependence is only 17%, while America reaches only 22%. In the process, China's living standard has improved greatly, which has also contributed to the economic growth of the surrounding countries. When the financial crisis broke out in East Asia in 1997 and 1998, China did not devaluate the RMB and made great contributions to enable the East Asian economy to overcome the financial crisis and restore its stability and growth.

In the recent years, some foreign economists and media have questioned the validity of rapid economic growth in China. After 1999 and 2000, some speculated that China's may be lying about its economic growth rate. This idea was first proposed by Thomas Rawski, a scholar on Chinese economy from the University of Pittsburgh in the U.S., which caught the attention of the media. Later, Lester C. Thurow, a very distinguished scholar from the Massachusetts Institute of Technology (MIT), wrote an article and stated that China's economic growth rate after 1998 could not be 7.8%, but it would be only 2% at the maximum, and some believed that it may even be a negative growth. Why have there been so many doubts about China's economic growth in recent years? An important reason is that two new economic phenomena have emerged in China since 1998, which were not witnessed during rapid economic growth in developed countries.

What are these new economic phenomena? The first is deflation along with rapid economic growth, and the other is the decrease of energy consumption despite rapid economic growth.

2. Chinese Economy Should Not Be Viewed Based on the Current Theoretical Model

After 1998, a new economic phenomenon occurred, which had never before occurred in the reform and opening up — deflation.

In other countries, deflation occurs only during zero or negative economic growth, except when the government provides great financial support, the growth rate may be a little above zero. However, from 1998 to the present, despite the constant decrease of commodity prices, China's economic growth rate has reached 7.8%, regarded as the most rapid rate in the world during this period. How could China maintain such a rapid economic growth rate under deflation? China had seen a negative growth in energy consumption during 1997–1999. Under deflation, other countries suffered negative economic growth but the growth of energy consumption was high along with the economic growth, but China does not follow this way. That is why some foreign economists doubt the validity of China's statistics and believe that the growth rate of 7% or 8% announced by the Chinese government is not true.

Regarding the validity of the statistics, the author's opinion is that it is not easy to interpret China's statistics. The doubts of the foreign economists result from their interpretation of China using the current theoretical model. Since Chinese economy is a transforming economy, many current economic models are not applicable.

The deflation that has emerged in China in the past several years could be witnessed by anyone who shops in the stores.

Then, how could China maintain its rapid economic growth when other countries suffer negative economic growth under deflation? In America, Japan, and some other countries, the bubbles in the real estate and stock market would appear before deflation. In developed countries, common people, generally, invest their wealth in real estate and stock markets. When the economic bubble becomes more serious, anyone who invests in real estate or stocks would feel like a rich man and this would lead to the "wealth effect" in the consumption method. For example, 91% of Japanese domestic production at that time was utilized to satisfy domestic consumption. Based on large consumption, these people would invest more to meet the requirements of the high consumption led by the great wealth.

When the bubble in real estate and stock bursts, many people would lose their wealth and plunge into heavy debts, because most of them had bought houses by bank mortgage. Under these circumstances, the consumption would reduce and therefore the production capacity invested in the period of bubbles becomes the excessive production capacity, thus leading to reductions in investment. The national economy would weather zero or negative growth upon the reduction of both consumption and investment.

However, deflation in China since 1998 was not formed in this way, because no bubble in the stock and real estate markets collapsed in 1998. Then, why did deflation emerge in China? It resulted from the wave of constant investment that was led by Deng Xiaoping in 1992 in his South China Speech. China has experienced a very rapid growth in investments since 1978, with an annual growth rate of 19% from 1981 to 1985, 7% from 1986 to 1990, and as high as 36% from 1991 to 1995. In addition to domestic investments in various categories, the foreign investment had also developed at a very rapid growth. To be specific, the foreign capital had never accounted for more than 5% in total investment in China before 1992, but the proportion had jumped to 12% in 1993, 15% in 1994, and reached 22% in 2002. Owing to the rapid growth of both domestic and foreign investments, China has accumulated increased its production capacity rapidly. Take the state-owned economy, which has increased at a comparatively slow rate, as an example. If the production capacity in 1990 was accepted as 100, the production capacity of state-owned enterprises had reached 273 by 1995. In addition, the growth rate of non-state-owned enterprises, private enterprises, and three-capital enterprises (enterprises in the three forms of Sino-joint venture, cooperative business, and exclusively foreign-owned enterprises in China) had been more rapid. The production capacity of China had increased by more than two times in the four or five years after the South China Speech. Therefore, China had suddenly changed from the shortage economy under the planned economy to a surplus economy by 1996 and 1997.

How did it become a surplus economy? It was because the general consumption was restricted by the growth in incomes. In the previous several years, the income level increased by 7% each year, whereas the consumption increased by only 50% despite the 200% increase in the production capacity. China had suddenly changed from a shortage economy to a surplus economy. This situation would never occur in foreign countries, so they cannot interpret the results incurred by deflation in China. China's deflation, led by the sudden increase of the production capacity, would not lead to the wealth effect. Owing to no wealth effect, the growth of consumption maintained the previous rate, i.e., an annual growth between 7% and 8%. Since the production capacity increased at a very rapid growth rate, much higher than the growth of consumption, the consumption capacity could not match with the excessive production capacity, necessarily leading to deflation and constant reduction in commodity prices. The investment would be influenced by the excessive production capacity. Investments in the private economy have been weakening since 1998. The government has to adopt an active fiscal policy to maintain the economic growth under these circumstances. From 1998 to the present, the government has launched a national debt of long-term construction of 800 billion yuan to stimulate the investment. The foreign investment has continued to grow at a rapid speed, so the investment has maintained a growth rate of about 10% each year. Based on the growing consumption and investment, the economy can naturally maintain a growth rate of about 8% each year. Compared to foreign countries where the deflation appears because of a sudden decrease in consumption, China's deflation results from the sudden increase in the production capacity. Since the causes of deflation vary between different countries, China maintains a strong growth of national economy despite the reduction of the commodity price.

3. Grasping Slight Changes to Interpret the Chinese Economy

How to explain the negative growth of energy consumption in 1997–1999 together with the rapid economic growth?

My elder brother had invested in a medium-sized cement plant, with an annual output of 400,000 tons. Before my brother's cement plant was established, three small cement plants of vertical kiln, a very old and traditional technology, were running businesses there. The total output of the three cement plants was 180,000 tons. The new cement plant, with an annual output of 400,000 tons, consumes energies equal to only 70% of the three small cement plants. Therefore, the other three cement plants were shut down after the establishment of my brother's cement plant, owing to the double output and 70% of energy consumption of the new plant. This situation was commonly seen in 1996 and 1997.

In the 1980s, China was in the stage of shortage economy, where the products were sold out and people could not buy many things. Therefore, a very special phenomenon, called the township enterprise, occurred in the Chinese economy. Peasants with low capital, low technological level, and low product quality invested in the township enterprise, as it was considered the main method for the peasants to become rich. In a shortage economy, the township enterprises could sell their products despite the low investment, technology, and product quality. By mid-1990s, a surplus of production capacity was created by the rapid growth in investment. The excessive production capacity mostly included newly increased productivities of foreign-invested enterprises and private enterprises, which enjoy a higher technological level and product quality. Some enterprises had to quit production based on the surplus, so the township enterprises of low quality and technology and large energy consumption were the first to declare bankruptcy and close. Therefore, along with the rapid economic growth, the change of the production and technology structure would correspondingly reduce the energy use. Foreign scholars have not grasped the slight, but profound, changes of the Chinese economy, so they could not understand the rapid growth of China under deflation and the reduction of energy consumption along with the economic growth. Fundamentally speaking, it is because they do not interpret China as a transforming economy. The rapid economic growth in the previous 25 years and the recent five years after 1998 is absolutely true.

4. Maintaining Rapid Economic Growth in the Next Two Decades

The economic growth rate of China in the next one or two decades is a topic of growing interest worldwide. The author believes that China would maintain its economic growth rate similar to the previous 25 years, i.e., about 8% each year. Despite any fluctuation, it is very possible for China to maintain an annual growth rate between 8% and 10%.

Research should be done on the three important aspects on the long-term economic growth of a country. The first is the possibility of growth among key factors in the country. Among these factors, land would not increase and labor is limited by the population, so it is important to consider the speed of capital accumulation. The second is the possibility of upgrading the industrial structure. Although some of the factors are constant and cannot grow, the economy would still maintain growth when the factors have transferred from the production of products of comparatively low added value to products of higher added value. The third is the technology. The improvement in technologies would also lead to the economic development in the same industry.

5. Technology — The Most Important Aspect in the Long-Term Economic Growth of a Country

Firstly, the possibility of capital increase may be restricted by the technological change. Without the technological upgrading, constant increase in capital would reduce the investment returns and lower the willingness to invest. Therefore, investment willingness depends on the speed of the technological change.

Secondly, the possibility of a structural change is also restricted by the technological change. Without new technologies, the industrial department that produces products of higher added value would not emerge. A quicker technological change would lead to the constant emergence of new departments of higher added value. Technological changes include two methods: (i) invention and (ii) introduction. The gap in the income levels compared with developed countries is actually the gap in the technological levels.

An important question is which method should be adopted by the developing countries such as China. The cost is the key to the answer. The introduction of technologies would require lesser investment and suffer smaller risks. Whether a developing country can utilize the technological gap to promote economic development depends on whether it can utilize its technological gap to the developed countries, introduce technologies from foreign countries, and promote rapid technological innovation.

The author has conducted many researches, such as why Japan and Asia's "Four Little Dragons" can catch up with developed countries or reduce their gaps with developed countries. The author believes that the key lies in that they had properly utilized their comparative advantages in each development stage and introduced new technologies to promote economic development. How many new technologies did Japan or the "Four Little Dragons" invent before the 1980s? Their inventions only accounted for a small part of the total inventions.

It is actually the same with China. China was a closed economy before 1978 and therefore it invented technologies, instead of introducing them from the foreign countries. Although the inventions of satellites and atomic bombs had succeeded, they were too costly, contributing to the slow and low-quality economic development of China before 1978. After 1978, China started to open the economy and introduced new technologies from foreign countries, thus enabling rapid economic growth rate.

Another problem is that, though it is the correct way for China to introduce technologies in order to promote economic development after the reform, how long can China maintain its development in the same way?

Generally speaking, the theory can only tell whether the road map is correct or not, but the influence can only be estimated based on the experiences. Japan can be regarded as an example for comparison, because the current economy of China is similar to that of Japan around 1960. The comparison is conducted among indicators including the life expectancy, infant mortality rate, and the Engel's coefficient. Japan's life expectancy was 68 for men and 73 for women in 1960, compared to 68 and 72, respectively, of China in 2000. The infant mortality rate was 3.1% in Japan in 1960, compared to 3.1% in China in 2000. Japan's proportion of agriculture in GDP was 16.7% in 1960, compared to 15.9% of China in 2000. For the Engel's coefficient, 38.8 yuan out of each 100 yuan earned by urban population was utilized to buy food in Japan in 1960, compared to 39.2 yuan of China in 2000. These social indicators comprehensively reflect the development of these economies. The indicators show that China's economic development level mostly equaled that of Japan in 1960. Japan had started rapid economic growth since 1960 and sustained its growth for 30 years. Japan's per-capita income had caught up with America by 1988.

Of course, the author does not expect that China's per-capita income can catch up with America by 2030. However, based on Japan's experiences and the change in the value of RMB, it is possible for China's per-capita income to reach half of America. By then, since the Chinese population is five times that of America, the whole economic scale of China would be 2.5 times of America. China's market would be the biggest market of the world. All investors are looking forward to the market.

6. Where is Chinese Economy Headed?[1]

6.1. *Editor's note from the 21st Century Business Herald*

Economics is becoming the most coveted education area in China, and Chinese economists have gradually adjusted to living in the public eye. However, do Chinese economists know which way the Chinese economy is headed? Do Chinese economists only listen to the scholars who have studied abroad, the textbooks of Harvard University, and a complete set of western context system? Do Chinese economists need to worship Nobel Prize winners and ask their opinions on the various problems in China? What do Chinese economists have, except for neoclassical economics and John Maynard Keynes?

A new academic year has begun, and a new group of students have started their exploration in economics. This chapter has an interview with Lin Yifu, the Director of the China Center for Economic Research at Beijing University, to discuss on the development direction of the Chinese economics. In 2004, the China Center for Economic Research at Beijing University celebrated its 10th anniversary. In these 10 years, education in Chinese economics has developed very rapidly. Lin Yifu has explored the techniques economics education and recently published *On the Methodology of Economics* and *On the Strategies for Economic Development*. This interview includes his latest thinking on the education of Chinese economics.

6.2. *Interview with Lin Yifu on the way Chinese economics lead*

6.2.1. *Current situation and bottlenecks for economic education*

Lin Yifu's conversation with Yu Nan of the *21st Century Business Herald* on the current situation of the domestic system of education on economics is as follows:

21st Century Business Herald: What is your view on the current situation of the domestic system of education on economics?

---

[1]This chapter was published in the *21st Century Business Herald* on September 3, 2005.

Lin Yifu: Compared to the start of the reform and opening up, domestic education in economics has changed a great deal. Economics, especially modern economics, has changed from being criticized to becoming the key content of economics education in universities. I remember that, when we were studying modern economics in the 1980s, teachers would, by the end of the introduction, add criticisms to any theory. Many new problems had emerged during China's transformation from its planned economy system to a socialist market economy system. Since this could not be explained by the traditional political economics, modern economics had become an important supplement from the original source of criticism. Along with the deepening of reform and improving market economy system, modern economics has become the mainstream of domestic education in economics, and has emerged as one of the most popular subjects among university students. According to specific statistics, students of undergraduate and postgraduate courses in economics admitted by China Center for Economic Research at Beijing University (hereinafter called "Center") accounted for 19% of the undergraduates of Beijing University. If the students in the Department of Economics and the Guanghua School of Management (GSM) are included, the proportion would exceed one-third.

From the late 1970s to early 1980s, no textbook on modern economics could be found in China, and teachers used their own fragmented notes in classes. Currently, the Chinese have translated the most popular economics textbooks used in the American universities. The Chinese editions for many latest American textbooks are published in China within one year. The *Economic Science Westport* organized by Liang Jing has played a key role in the previous 10 years, while the Chinese Economists Society in America has made great contributions. The current textbooks for economics in domestic universities are no different from textbooks in the American universities.

Regarding the teachers, there were no teachers who returned to China after studying in western countries during the 1950s to late 1980s. Professors who came back to China before the 1950s were too old in the 1980s. Therefore, at the beginning of the reform and opening up, the teachers for modern economics were mostly transferred from theoretical history or traditional political economics, showing a gap in teacher supply. The Center was the first institution to attract the overseas Chinese students to return back to China. By now, there are several talented economic teachers from foreign countries. The Center is not the only institution that attracts students back to China. The GSM, Qinghua, Zhejiang University, Fudan University, Zhongshan University, and Nankai University, etc., saw more teachers returning to China after studying abroad.

The above facts indicate the huge and profound changes in China in domestic economics education in the previous 20 years.

Lin Yifu's answers to the question "what are the bottlenecks for education in economics?" in his interview with Yu Nan of the *21st Century Business Herald* is as follows:

21st Century Business Herald: According to you, what are the bottlenecks for education in economics? What is the main factor that restricts the current domestic system of education in economics?

Lin Yifu: Before I answer that question, the goal of research and education in economics should be clarified first. Does the research and education on economics aim to study only the theory, or understand and positively affect the society?

Economics became an independent subject of social science after Adam Smith's *The Wealth of Nations* was published in 1997. In my opinion, economics has always been an applicable science aiming to understand, transform, and facilitate the development of society and influence common people's selection of consumption, investment, and employment as well as the national policies. The characteristic is reflected by the full name of *The Wealth of Nations, An Inquiry into the Nature and Causes of the Wealth of Nations*. The department of economics at the University of Chicago was famous for its academic style, where professors seldom took on administrative roles. However, when Professor Gary Becker at the University of Chicago came to the Center for the "HSBC Lecture by Economics Nobel Prize Winner", he was asked whether professors at the University of Chicago paid attention only to the perfection of theories, but disregarded the practical value of theories. He answered that professors at the University of Chicago, including Friedman, Schurz, Stigler, Lucas, and himself, conducted research with the goal to understand the results of personal selections and governmental policies and further influence the personal selections and governmental policies.

However, economists deduce any theoretical position of modern economics based on certain theoretical models. This indicates how the policy makers make the best selection under certain constraint conditions, while the selection is the object of studies. Owing to personal restrictions, economists cannot guarantee that the constraint conditions in the theoretical model are exactly the most important constraint conditions for the policy makers in the real society. In addition, for the same problems to be solved, the most important constraint conditions may vary in different countries, societies, and policy makers. The constraint conditions may be different at different stages even for the same person. Therefore, there is no theory that can be applied universally in economics.

The research center of modern economics is located in the U.S., so theoretical research in modern economics is mainly directed toward the economic phenomena in developed countries, as represented by the U.S. These theories may not be applicable for transforming and developing countries such as China. Although some American and European economists put forth efforts to study the problems of developing and transforming countries, they cannot properly handle the main constraint conditions for developing and transforming countries without their own experiences and often come to ineffective conclusions. According to the mainstream theories of economics in the 1950s and 1960s, the countries that formulated development policies had encountered various difficulties in economic development in the 1970s and could not carry on with their development programs. In the 1980s and 1990s, development and socialist countries had carried out reform and transformation in succession, while those that made policies according to the "Washington Consensus" formed by the mainstream theories of economics at that time had come to the unexpected disastrous results.

Therefore, I think that the main bottleneck for China's current education system in economics lies in the lack of theories and systems that could help understand and provide solutions to solving the problems in the development and reform of the Chinese economy, with the real problems in the economic development and reform of China as the object of studies. Most textbooks regard foreign phenomena as the object of studies. As the present education does not meet the reality, because of the lack of these theories and systems, some students and even some teachers misinterpret the goal of such education as the perfection of theories and regard economics education as a kind of education on ideology.

6.2.2. *Study local problems with a normative approach*

Lin Yifu's opinions to solve the bottlenecks in economics education are as follows:

21st Century Business Herald: Then, how to solve the "bottleneck" you mentioned?

Lin Yifu: As early as the founding of the Center in 1995, I wrote an article entitled *Localization, Normalization, and Internationalization* to celebrate the 40th anniversary of *Economic Studies*, to state my opinion on the research and education on economics and its striving direction.

I believe that although no theory can be applied universally, the research approach for economics can be the same. I agree with Gary Becker, the 1992 Nobel Prize winner, that economics is distinguished from other social studies for the method of problem analysis in economics. The economists study problems and construct the theory based on the assumption that policy makers are "rational", which, in my opinion, means that "the policy maker will always make the best choice within the selection scope". When making choices, the selection scopes may vary owing to different constraint conditions, such as the status of the policy makers, the development stage of the country, and the social systems, so the best choice may vary. Economic theories, including the frontier theories, enable resolve policy makers' problems by considering important constraints, and provide best choice and a form of expression of the rational principle under certain conditions. As economic theories are applied widely, Chinese economists should commit themselves to researching on the problems of the Chinese economy. As long as the policy makers behind the economic phenomena are rational, the studies on local problems, with a rigorous and normative approach, can reach a result as good as the achievements made by the same approach to study the problems of developed countries. No matter whether they are local problems or problems of developed countries, both the studies have contributed to world economics, helped people to understand the unknown economic phenomena, increased the knowledge of the people to solve real economic problems, and facilitated globalization.

In 11 years, the Center has gathered a group of scholars who train in modern economics concepts and also understand Chinese practices. Such scholars, it is expected, would exert efforts according to the above direction, study Chinese economic problems in a rigorous method of economics, and educate and encourage our students with researches on the economic problems in China.

The Center's role in solving the new problems in the reform, openness, and development of China as explained by Lin Yifu is as follows:

21st Century Business Herald: What has the Center achieved?

Lin Yifu: The following aspects are included: For example, Cai Chuang, Li Zhou, myself, other partners, and some students have constructed a comparatively complete theoretical system for the development and transformation of China. These were made according to the concept of economic development proposed by China's transformation and development, with the viability of enterprises as the micro foundation and building the comparative advantage in factor endowment structure and improving the structure as the goal. This theoretical system can basically explain the "behind the scenes" stories for the administrative distortion in foreign trade, finance, industrial structure, and labor market in China and many developing countries; the corruptions; unfair income distribution; and crony capitalism commonly seen in many developing and transforming countries, and the reasons why the evolutionary reform is more effective than reform by "shock therapy".

Moreover, Professor Zhou Qiren has conducted an in-depth and systematic elaboration on China's reform and development from the perspective of the property rights. Professor Lu Feng has given a comparatively complete explanation on the transformation of international trade from an original product-oriented trade to a trade mainly of finer components within the products, from the perspectives of technological progress and lower transaction fees. Professor Chen Ping has criticized and amended Lucas's rational expectation theory upon the combination of the current chaos theory in terms of methodology. Meanwhile, our students try to explain the realistic problems in the reform and development of China in their thesis, such as the soft budget constraints, income difference, and direction and results of labor flow, based on both theoretical model and empirical test.

Of course, since the Center has only been founded for 11 years, it can be said that our teachers and students have made a spectacular beginning in solving the new problems in the reform, openness, and development of China. Joint efforts among educational and research institutes and generations of economists are needed to overcome the "bottleneck" in China's economics education.

6.2.3. *Economic analysis and mathematical tools*

Lin Yifu's views on the relationship between economics and mathematics in his interview with Yu Nan of the *21st Century Business Herald* are as follows:

21st Century Business Herald: Some economists affirm that economics is moving toward the no-return road in mathematics. How do you view the relationship between economics and mathematics?

Lin Yifu: Firstly, I should clarify the foundation and results of economics researches before I answer this question. The opinion appears before the logical system for the research and analysis of economics. Actually, scholars who had received education in economics from the top research universities in America know that the intuition on the reasons leading to the occurrence of the problem is very important in economics research. Traditional American dictionary defines intuition defined as "the behavior or ability to acquire knowledge or feeling without inference or the use of reason". In order to study a problem, an economist firstly judges the reasons for the phenomenon by intuition and then presents his or her opinion with rigorous logic. The mathematical model is one method, but not the only method, of logical representation. If the ability to establish a model with mathematics is a necessary condition for economists, then even Adam Smith, David Ricardo, Friedrich Hayek, Ronald Coase, and Douglass North cannot be regarded as economists. In addition to this, the mathematical model can hardly be utilized to propose useful theories, because the mathematical model may infer different conclusions according to different constraint conditions.

In the research of economic problems, intuition is the foundation and the mathematical tool is the result. Economics education should not only emphasize the importance of mathematical tools but also attach more importance to economic intuition. Economic intuition is derived from a comprehensive understanding and experience of society, economy, history, culture, and methodology of economics. Students of art hold some advantages in intuition and would not stronger in the study of economics, even if they are not good at mathematics. In addition, many researches on economic problems can be clarified without the mathematical model. *21st Century Business Herald*: Then, why is mathematics so important in current economics?

Lin Yifu: Of course, mathematics is the most precise logic. Except experts in economics, common people cannot be precise, based on the logic of language. The deduction based on the mathematical model can effectively avoid the logical mistakes and easily discover any mistakes. For example, Professor Huo Deming, a new addition to our Center, once revealed Lucas's mistake of mathematical logic in a ground article written in the 1980s. Therefore, the application of mathematics is required by the rigorous economics system.

Why does mathematics currently takes precedence over other aspects of economics? The research center of economics was located in Great Britain in the 18th and 19th centuries and was later transferred to the U.S. after 1930 — always located in the most advanced economy. However, the countries of most advanced market economies only saw an annual economic growth rate of 2% after the Industrial Revolution, compared to 9% and 10% of developing countries. The developed countries, with a stable society, have not given rise to many new and major economic and social phenomena. Therefore, after initiative researches on major economic phenomena were conducted by scholars at the early stages, such as Adam Smith, only a few economic and social phenomena have been included in research. Subsequently, economists only research some minor phenomena and propose minor theories or research as the supplement and amendments to the main theoretical models. How are the contributions made by this research to be evaluated? They are actually techniques, instead of explanations, on economic phenomena.

21st Century Business Herald: Do you mean that, since no big issue can be researched, everyone has to compete in the technical details?

Lin Yifu: Yes. It is also related to the advancements in modern economics in the west. Similar to the U.S., there are over 50,000 economists and more than 10,000 teaching staffs in the universities in China. These 10,000 economists have to present papers each year for endurance and promotion, but there are not enough phenomena for researches. They have to work hard on their techniques. Also, owing to the large number of economists, the esteemed universities place mathematics as the threshold for hiring professors.

21st Century Business Herald: How does the Center place emphasis on mathematics? How do you consider the position of mathematics?

Lin Yifu: It is best for students to give attention to both the foundation and results. Additional learning on mathematics would enable them to cross the threshold to become economists. If they fail in crossing the threshold, then it would be difficult for them to publish articles and be accepted by other economists. Especially, we are studying on Chinese problems, which Americans have little understanding, so we have to use the mathematical model to obtain worldwide concern and acknowledge. However, we emphasize that mathematics is only a tool, and we should utilize the tools, but not be restricted by the tools. The observation and analysis ability for problems, as well as the intuition of economics should be emphasized. This is why I attach much attention to methodology on classes and publish my dialogs with students on methodology.

6.2.4. *Chinese problems are frontier problems*

The frontier problems in economics as listed by Lin Yifu in his interview with Yu Nan of the *21st Century Business Herald* are as follows:

21st Century Business Herald: What are the frontier problems in economics?

Lin Yifu: The frontier problems of economics are distinguished from the frontier points of natural science, such as physics and chemistry. The theories of physics and chemistry generally develop in a straightforward way, while new research results are often established based on the progress on previous research achievements. However, economics develops by negating, instead of inheriting, the previous theories.

Take development economics as an example. The neoclassical growth theory dominating the 1960s and 1970s considered that the per-capita incomes of developed and developing countries would get closer, and the final economic growth rate of all countries would be equal to the population growth rate. The neoclassical growth theory believed that since the technologies of all countries were externally given at the same level, the gap in per-capita incomes between developed and developing countries was derived from the held per-capita capital. The new growth theory maintained the idea of the neoclassical growth theory that all technologies of all countries are equal, but they believe that technologies are internally supported by investments.

The reason to abandon the neoclassical growth theory is that the gap of per-capita incomes between developed and developing countries had not narrowed, but had widened, after World War II (WWII). In addition, the economic growth rate of developed countries exceeded the population growth rate. The new growth theory was not built based on the neoclassical theory, but changed the prerequisite and assumption for the neoclassical growth theory. According to the new growth theory, the growth rate of developed countries exceeding the growth rate of population results from developed countries' constant investment on technological innovation. The increasing gap of the per-capita income between developing and developed countries is because of the decreased investments in technological innovation in developing countries than developed countries.

The new growth theory had been popular from the mid-1980s to the mid-1990s, but it could not explain why the East Asian economy had seen an economic growth rate that was higher than the developed countries and how it narrowed the gap of per-capita income with, or even caught up with, the developed countries, as its investment on technological innovation was far less than the developed countries. Daron Acemoglu and others from Harvard and MIT, at the frontier of development economics, have researched most of the external variables for the long-term growth of a country's economy. For example, how did the differences in the climate and mortality rate between Central and South America and North America affect the economic growth when the colonization of the U.S. began 300 or 400 years ago?

Take the macroeconomic theory as another example. In May 2005, I attended an international meeting for the celebration of the 55th anniversary of a bank in South Korea to discuss on the latest progress in the theories of financial and monetary policies. I mainly studied the development, transformation, and agriculture and have no knowledge of the macroeconomic theory. In the meeting, I found that many conclusions of the rational expectancy theory, the most frontier theory in the 1980s when I studied at the University of Chicago, had been abandoned or amended, and the most popular theories were new Keynesianism and neoclassical synthesis theory.

The rational expectancy theory had negated (a) Keynesianism's opinion that the governmental financial policies were effective and (b) the idea of the Phillips Curve (that a substitute relation existed between the inflation rate and unemployment rate). These were negated, because they could not explain the stagflation in the 1970s, while the rational expectancy theory was amended, and because it could not explain the significant influence of the monetary policies adopted by central banks of countries in the counter economic cycle.

In brief, the economic theories often develop by negating the previous theories, instead of absorbing the previous theoretical results. Because the old theories cannot explain the new phenomena, new theories appear, negate the previous theories, build a new theoretical model based on new assumptions, and clarify the new causality.

21st Century Business Herald: What are the current frontier problems of economics?

Lin Yifu: Personally, I believe that problems in China are the most frontier problems in economics. As many phenomena in China's reform and development cannot be explained with the current mainstream theory, the new theories proposed based on the studies on these new phenomena are the new and frontier theories. The frontier problems are not the only problems that have been researched by economists from famous American universities. Of course, the current research center of economics is still located in America, so problems researched by economists from famous universities in America can easily obtain concern from the international economic circle.

It is both a responsibility and a very rare opportunity for the Chinese economists to study the economic problems in China. Most economic researchers are the elite among the Chinese, who share imperative responsibilities for the country and society. In order to promote the economic development, they should deepen their researches on China's issues and propose theories that can explain and solve China's economic issues.

Since Adam Smith, the research center of the world economics has always been combined with the world economic center. Along with China's economic development, China is enjoying a higher economic status in international economy, so the international economic circle would give more attention to research in China. Any economic theory is built upon economists' intuition on the economic phenomena, so Chinese economists share the advantage of being in a favored position. As long as the Chinese economy develops at a rapid rate, we would definitely usher in the new international trend of economics where many masters would stand out in China.

21st Century Business Herald: Then, what preparations should Chinese students make to study the Chinese economic problem, the frontier problem of economics?

Lin Yifu: Firstly, they should cultivate their intuitions on economics. Owing to tens of thousands of social and economic variables, if any variable maintained in the model is false, it cannot reveal the real cause for the phenomenon under research. In addition, if more variables are kept in the model, the model would become very complicated and may not reach a determining result. However, the economic phenomenon to be explained has been confirmed. The difference between a expert and a mediocre economist lies in that the expert can figure out which is the most important factor contributing to the phenomenon, which variables should be given up, and which variables should be maintained in the theoretical model, upon only a look at the phenomenon.

In order to cultivate good economic intuitions, economic researchers should learn the research approach of economics and develop a humanistic quality and a profound understanding of Chinese history, culture, and society. Since economic phenomena often takes place in reality, the variable that is important for the western countries, and should be maintained in the theoretical model, may not be that important in China owing to different development stages, cultural traditions, and social systems. The importance of a variable cannot only be inferred from the mathematical model, but it should also be explored by personal understanding in the society. It is difficult for us to grasp the opportunity conferred by experience without good humanistic quality.

Secondly, a favorable mathematical basis is important, which would enable us to present our economic intuitions with a rigorous mathematical model and inspect the deductions of the theoretical model with a precise calculation. It is the threshold for us to join the club of the international economics circle, only by which we would have the opportunity to influence the international economics circle.

6.2.5. *Explore the discourse space of Chinese economics*

The two important aspects of the discourse power of the west as presented by Lin Yifu in his interview with Yu Nan of the *21st Century Business Herald* are as follows:

21st Century Business Herald: You believe that the problems in the Chinese economy are the frontier problems, but how is the discourse space of Chinese economics to be created, if the west still leads the discourse power?

Lin Yifu: The following two aspects mainly present the discourse power of the west you mentioned. Firstly, issues that western scholars are more concerned may not be the most important issues for China, such as the elections, human rights, intellectual property rights, minority nationalities, and women's rights. We do not mean that these issues are not important in China, but they are currently not the main conflict and problem in the Chinese society.

Secondly, we utilize theories and concepts in our analysis of problems, so it is common that we accept what is considered as the important issue in the western concept, and ignore what is not included in the western concept. Western scholars may accept our analysis of Chinese problems based on western theories and concepts. However, the phenomena in China may be the same with the west, but the "behind the scenes" stories are completely different.

For example, the manifestations of China's deflation between 1998 and 2002 and developed countries' deflation (the constant decline of the commodity price) are the same. However, the developed countries' deflation was incurred by the collapse of the bubbles in stock and real estate markets and the wealth effect, which led to consumption decline, excessive production capacity, and weak economic growth, in addition to the constant decline in commodity prices. However, China's deflation was created by the overheating investment during previous times and sharp growth in production capacity, which led to excessive production capacity and decline in commodity prices, but no wealth effect. Also, deflation did not influence the consumption, and the consumption maintained a similar growth rate as before. The investment on private economy decreased, owing to the excessive production capacity, but the government adopted robust financial policies to maintain a certain growth rate of investment.

Based on the continuous growth of consumption and investment, China maintained rapid economic growth, despite the decline in the commodity price. However, countries of developed market economy have never before seen the co-existence of the deflation and high economic growth, so foreign economists seriously doubt about China's high economic growth rate under deflation. Moreover, Chinese scholars may prescribe for China's deflation according to the foreign theory on deflation. However, the theoretical model and prescriptions may vary owing to different causes for deflation. In addition, some new analysis concepts are be proposed. For example, the excessive production capacity refers to the stock of production capacity that is not used, so the best method to deal with deflation is to stimulate the stock demands. However, most people become used to considering problems based on current theories and concepts, and the new theories and concepts proposed according to China's phenomena can hardly be accepted by the domestic and foreign academic circles.

However, it is not only the new theories on Chinese economy proposed upon the research that can hardly be accepted by the academic circle. This is because most people have become used to their previous "habits of mind" in studying the theories, and it becomes difficult even for an economist to persuade another economist who has already accepted a totally different theory. When an economist proposes new theories, he or she does not aim to persuade the economists that have already accepted the current theories, but he or she exerts influence on new students of this field. For example, Lucas's rational expectancy theory was basically not accepted by the economics circle and he was attacked by many people when he presented his paper at Harvard University, Yale University, and Princeton University. However, this theory could explain the stagflation that was not explained by the old Keynesianism. As a result, the rational expectancy theory of Lucas was accepted by more and more students and it became the new mainstream theory.

The new theories and concepts proposed upon China's phenomena are in a more difficult position than Lucas'. The "Washington Consensus", which was established in the current mainstream system of theories and concepts, is the current mainstream idea in economics on the reasons and solutions to problems of developing and transforming countries.

The phenomena that are not seen in mainstream theoretical frame and ideas are ignored, which may be the more fundamental factors contributing to the problems in developing and transforming countries. For example,

I believe that the fundamental reason for governmental interference and system distortion of developing and transforming countries lies in that the government wants to support the enterprises of advanced technologies, intensive capitals, disagreement with the comparative advantages, and no viability in the competing market. However, enterprises without viability are rarely seen in developed countries, so the mainstream economics does not incorporate the concept of viability and proposes theories based on the assumption that all enterprises are equipped with viability. The domestic academic circle often analyzes domestic problems based on foreign theories and concepts. Therefore, in order to generate influence in China, the theories should firstly exert influence in the foreign countries. When Lucas proposed the rational expectancy theory, western economists had some understanding about western social, cultural, and economic phenomena, but Chinese economy, society, and culture are distinguished from the west, making it more difficult to persuade foreign economists. Before the Chinese people start accepting the new theories and concepts proposed by the domestic and foreign academic circles, they need to overcome their mental block in following the previous theories and concepts and they should also become familiar with the Chinese social and economic phenomena. The relevant articles can be hardly published by mainstream magazines.

However, the most important responsibility of economists is not to publish articles in the mainstream magazines, but to explain the concerning phenomenon and contribute to the theoretical development of economics, with more theoretical explanations proposed. The theories would be gradually accepted only if they can explain the phenomena. Along with China's economic development, foreign economic circles show more and more concern for China's problems and would accept more theoretical explanations proposed upon Chinese phenomena since they cannot explain these problems with their own theories. The current status can be gradually and imperceptibly changed. Opportunities and difficulties often coincide. Figuratively, the Chinese economic phenomenon is a gold mine. Therefore, the key problem does not lie in whether the new theories and concepts proposed can be accepted by domestic and foreign academic circles, but whether we can be free from the restrictions by the current concepts and theories, as well as the discourse hegemony, and propose new theories and concepts based on China's phenomena. Therefore, in the dialog in *On Methodology of Economics*, I particularly emphasized that scholars should conduct researches on the phenomena and problems with an attitude of "no thinking".

21st Century Business Herald: Under the strong western discourse power, how can we get rid of the restrictions by the current concepts and theories, as well as the discourse hegemony?

Lin Yifu: This question relates to the true nature of economics. A discourse background would appear as economics is considered a set of existing theories, because all theories are proposed to understand a certain phenomenon of a certain society. Similar to the Chinese phenomena being unfamiliar to foreign economists, these phenomena would be unfamiliar to us. As mentioned before, for the analysis and study of problems, the theories of economics share the same methodology that "the policy maker will always make the best choice within the selection scope", which can be applied universally, to China or foreign countries, in ancient or modern times.

For example, in the age of planned economy, the best choice for members in the agricultural production teams of distribution, according to work, is to slacken in their jobs due to the difficulty in supervision. The same situation also existed in ancient China, when the well-field system was adopted. It was recorded in Lüshi Chunqiu[2] that according to different system arrangements, producers would make their best choices under the weak supervision. The famous ancient story of Mr. Nan Guo[3] also reflects

---

[2] A famous Chinese classic recorded Lv Buwei's commentaries of the history.

[3] This story is set in the Warring States period of Chinese history. In this period, there was a state called Qi and the King of Qi was very fond of music and so he had a special orchestra to entertain him. Being a musician in this orchestra was a highly sought after job. This is because the king gave very special consideration to the musicians and also treated them quite well. The king was very fond of listening to the music played on the yu. On hearing this, a man named Nan Guo wanted to become a member of the orchestra and he bought his own yu. But the problem was that he could not play the yu. He was somewhat brazen and boasted to the king that he could play the yu. The king was very happy to add more musicians to his orchestra and so he admitted Nan Guo in his orchestra. The king did not even ask him to play the yu before he admitted him in his orchestra. During every practice, Nan Guo pretended to play the yu and tried to imitate what the other musicians were doing. He moved his head in time according to the music and put on his best act as if he knew what he was doing. Nan Guo was doing this for several years successfully that the king never suspected anything. Later, the king died and the prince ascended the throne. The prince also loved to listen to the yu, but his preferences were different from his father. He thought that the sound of 300 people playing together was much too loud. So the new king issued a

the same phenomenon. I believe that the economic theories can be applied universally to analyze Chinese phenomena, and it is not difficult for the Chinese to accept. The theories are presentations of the methodology in a certain situation, where a certain discourse environment exists. Quite a few theories that are popular in the west are unfamiliar and are even difficult for us to understand.

21st Century Business Herald: Should the education on economics be totally westernized or combined with Chinese practices?

Lin Yifu: Obviously, the answer to this question is based on my opinions on the previous questions that the domestic system of economics education should be carried out based on the Chinese practices. The current mainstream theory is the result of the application of economic theories in countries of advanced market economy. These theories are useful for interpreting and solving the phenomena and problems of developed countries, but the theories themselves are not the truth.

It is certain that, along with the development and variations in social and economic phenomena of developed countries, the current mainstream theories would be amended or even abandoned. China's problems are somewhat different from developed countries that boast of market economy, so it is a dogmatizing and ideological behavior to simply apply the mainstream theories in China. Since the time of Adam Smith, economics has been a subject that governed and benefited the people. Only the theories proposed upon Chinese practices could help us understand and solve the problems in China. Therefore, in order to contribute to China's reform and development, education in economics should cultivate the students to view and analyze problems based on the methodology of economics and teach students with theories that are proposed upon Chinese practices. Only then, students can understand the theories profoundly and can apply these theories in their practical work. A tradition in the department of economics of the University of Chicago is that foreign students should write their doctoral thesis on the domestic problems prevailing in their country. It is because theories are utilized only to explain the practical problems, whereas the cultural background forms the base for understanding the practical

---

decree: all 300 musicians were to practice very well, and then each one would play for the king individually. When Nan Guo heard this, he packed his things and left the court.

problems. This helps in writing better theses and enables the students to carry out research in their homeland. This method should be learned from the China's education in economics.

6.2.6. *From learning the truth from the west to localization*

Lin Yifu lists the development course of Chinese economics in terms of the history in his interview with Yu Nan of the *21st Century Business Herald* as follows:

21st Century Business Herald: What is the development course of Chinese economics in terms of the history?

Lin Yifu: The development course of Chinese economics would definitely shift from learning the truth from the west to localization, such as the Buddhism in China. Buddhism was introduced to China during the Eastern Han Dynasty. At the beginning, Buddhism was mainly disseminated by the translation of western Buddhist classics and only exerted influence on the upper class. It was not until the Sixth Patriarch Huineng — which localized the western Buddhism in the Tang Dynasty — that Buddhism started to generate great influence on the Chinese society. China started to make great contributions to the development of Buddhism and Buddhism became popular among all ranks and also became an integral part of the Chinese cultural traditions.

Economics has become an independent social subject since the publication of *The Wealth of Nations* by Adam Smith. After this publication, the research center of economics was firstly located in Britain and then in America. Under these circumstances, China had to introduce the subject, economics, first. However, theories only hold under certain space–time conditions. The rational principle is universal for all theories of economics. We have to think about how to utilize the methodology of economics to analyze the problems and cultivate the economic intuition by combining the understanding on Chinese society. Then, we can propose the theories and systems to explain and solve China's problems according to China's phenomena. Since 1901 when Yan Fu translated and published *The Wealth of Nations*, the Chinese first learned from the theories of western economics and hoped that they could make their country stronger by changing the prevailing poor and backward situations in China. However, the theories of the western economics cannot be applied universally. China's economics should develop in the road of localization based on theoretical innovations, thus enabling contributions to the development of China. Then, Chinese economists can contribute to the world economics.

21st Century Business Herald: Buddhism is actually closer to human nature and may arouse more responses. In economics, theories are proposed based on the facts. Will it be more difficult to localize economics since China has, for a long time, learned from the west?

Lin Yifu: The *Diamond Sutra*, a well-known Buddhist classic, has well answered this question. All Buddhist sayings are laws preached by Buddha to help people attain Nirvana. A total of about 84,000 Buddhist philosophies were taught. Each philosophy directs against the people under a certain situation, but means nothing to the people under another situation. Meanwhile, all these philosophies are the paths to Nirvana. The question is whether people can or cannot become a Buddhist by practicing these 84,000 kinds of principles. The answer is No. Problems are constantly changing, so the situation of a person may be different from the 84,000 kinds of principles mentioned by Buddha. Therefore, the Zen Buddhism emphasized self-enlightenment, seeking Buddha within the heart.

The existing theories of economics can be compared to the principles of Buddhism. We can only learn how to use the methodology of economics in specific situations by learning from the theories proposed upon the facts of the west, but should not directly imitate these theories. Based on China's practical problems, we need to propose new theories in order to solve the problems in China. Until the localized theoretical system of China is completed, the theories in textbooks would be necessarily derived from the facts of the west. Even if the theoretical system of China has matured and the theories in the textbooks are proposed based on China's facts, we should also utilize the same attitude in the system. As Confucius had once stated about the time flow, the world is constantly changing and any theory proposed is "about the thing that happened before". We should not regard the existing theories as the truth that we must follow. If we can maintain our rational attitude in this way, learning theories proposed upon the facts of the west would not inhibit the localization of economics.

21st Century Business Herald: How can Chinese economists become experts in the subject? Will it be possible for any Chinese economist to win the Nobel Prize?

Lin Yifu: I have indicated on many occasions that there would be many experts in economics appearing in China in the near future. Economic theories are derived from economic phenomenon, and the contributions to economic theories depend on the importance of the phenomenon to be explained. What is the most important economic phenomenon? The economic phenomenon occurs only in the most important country. Chinese economy is playing an increasingly important role in the world economics because of its rapid economic growth rate. Owing to this, the researches and theories on China's economic problems would exert greater influence in world economics circle. Therefore, many Chinese economists may become leaders in world economics.

At least two generations' worth of effort is necessary for the possibility of a Chinese economist to win a Nobel Prize. This generation of economists had to turn from learning the truth from the west to the consensus on localization of education and researches on economics. This is already a positive result. If the consensus and efforts had commenced earlier, the next generation of economists, i.e., present students, may have the chance to become the masters of the international economics circle. Yes, it is possible for them to win the Nobel Prize for economics.

7. What Kind of MBA Education Does China Need?[4]

7.1. *Introduction: Emergence of the problem*

Ling Zhijun has written an engaging and detailed account of Lenovo — who, in 20 years, has all the experiences that local enterprises may encounter. Lenovo is featured with all Chinese characteristics of this period. At the beginning, Lenovo made great efforts to place the company under the Institute of Computing Technology Chinese Academy of Science to establish the company's authority and validity. The company sought for their first dollar in the "gray area" and found their springboard under policies and power. The company also experienced personnel transition in its most

---

[4]This chapter was published in the *21st Century Business Review* 6th issue 2005, interviewed by Yu Nan.

splendid stage. The famous "battle between Liu and Ni",[5] can hardly be merely summarized as the conflict between technicians and capitalists. Finally, the important personnel of Lenovo, Yang Yuanqing and Guo Wei, respectively, started their own businesses, which indicated the balance of benefits in employment uniquely seen among the Chinese entrepreneurs.

Compared to the story of the Microsoft Company, written by the same author, the story of Lenovo is not as exciting and attractive, but shows some of China's realities. Common readers can feel the helplessness, compromise, and setbacks in the development of Lenovo. It also demonstrates that not all excellent talents can play their role in the talent mechanism, and their destinies are affected by the opportunities and restrictions in China's development and transformation and the practical demands of the enterprise at that time.

Not all Chinese enterprises share the same experiences as Lenovo, but they have to respond to social development for survival. Entrepreneurs and managers can only be great men by understanding the times.

This is the background for China's MBA education. Can an MBA help entrepreneurs and managers clear away the haze in the rapid reform of Chinese society and precisely seize the pulse of the times?

7.2. China's MBA education is in need of new models

In the west, MBA, representing the technological management, has created great profits for enterprises. MBA has quickly obtained high reputation since its introduction in China, because of China's aspiration for advanced management technologies and experience. However, as MBA is conferred with honor in China, the trained experts of management technologies often face difficulties when settling into their new roles as enterprise leaders in China.

Our interview with Professor Lin Yifu, the Director of the China Center for Economic Research of Beijing University, was conducted with these doubts on the current MBA education in China. The Beijing University International MBA (BiMBA) won the "MBA of Most Market Value of

---

[5]Two leading figures of Lenovo, Liu Chuanzhi and Ni Guangnan, came to serious disagreements in 1994. The general engineer, Ni Guangnan, advocated to head on the technical route and put main efforts on chips; but chairman Liu Chuanzhi proposed to give full play to the cost advantage of China's manufacturing and put more efforts to build the China-made brand.

China" in the 2005 survey of the business and management education as published in *Wealth* (Chinese edition). Why does the MBA, organized by a research center with economic research as the main task, stand out in so many MBA projects and lead the MBA organized by commercial colleges and schools of management in the evaluation by *Wealth* and other institutions?

Professor Lin pointed out that the Chinese should rely on "good timing, favorable geographical position, and good human relations" to do anything well. In terms of business management, the human relations refer to the internal management, i.e., how to stimulate the enthusiasm of the staff to jointly strive for the enterprises' goals; the favorable geographical position here refers to the correct position of enterprises, how to make full use of local advantages, and improve the market competitiveness of enterprises; and the good timing refers to the opportunities and challenges on the survival and development of enterprises created by the variation of the social structure and institutional environment. MBA education originated in developed countries of market economy with stable social structure and institutional environment, so foreign scholars on management studies do not pay much attention to the good timing, but attach importance to the favorable geographical position and good human relations. They emphasize on how to strengthen the internal management, establish the rational excitation mechanism, and expand and develop enterprises, but ignore the education on how to adapt to the variation of social structure and institutional environment and the opportunities brought about by the reform. Since China is a transforming and developing country under rapid economic growth, the social structure and institutional environment of China have been constantly changing, leading to various business opportunities and traps. The senior executive of an enterprise should be capable of dealing with the variation, seizing the opportunities, handling the challenges, and avoiding the traps. These are the most important qualities for good entrepreneurs in transforming and developing countries.

What the foreign MBA education lacks is exactly the strong point of the Center. Since the establishment of the Center in 1994, its key responsibilities have been to conduct research, participate in various developmental programs and reforms, and promote the economic reform and development of China. All professors of the Center have accepted complete education on economics and management studies overseas, but the characteristic of the Center lies in that each professor has experienced China's profound institutional reform. Since more than half of the professors in the Center had been the educated youths who were sent to the rural areas for gaining experiences, they could understand the true status of the bottom of China's society. Meanwhile, they were also the initial beneficiaries from the end of the Cultural Revolution and the restoration of the entrance examination in the university. Several of them have been actively involved in the formulation of policies for the social and economic system reform since the early 1980s, and continued to participate and promote many important reforms after they returned to China in the early 1990s completing their studies overseas. In addition, they did not simply imitate the mainstream theories of foreign countries that then existed, but summarized and reached new theories that could explain and estimate the social reforms of China based on their in-depth understanding of Chinese realities. Since the initiation of BiMBA, its guiding principle has been to combine the education on the social and institutional reform of China and foreign management education, which has been warmly welcomed by MBA students from the very beginning. In the courses of BiMBA, the most popular and highly appraised lessons include the Institutional Environment for Business Activities in China by Professor Zhou Qiren and the Economic Reform and Development of China by Professor Lin Yifu. Professor Zhou Qiren has delivered his personal interpretation of economic theories and understanding of Chinese economic phenomena, and Professor Lin Yifu has taught students with his profound understanding of the basic theories of economics and broad and special visual angles on domestic and foreign economic developments. MBA students, i.e., entrepreneurs and managers, have benefited a great deal from each of their lessons, when China's correct development path has been pointed out.

The innovation of the model of BiMBA organized by the Center is undoubtedly the reason why BiMBA ranks first against many other institutions in the evaluation conducted by *Wealth*. The innovation of BiMBA's model also creates an example of a new model that can be learnt by MBA education projects in China and other transforming and developing countries. The MBA education that focuses on "good timing, favorable geographical position, and good human relations" is more suited for the demands of senior executives in the rapidly reforming and developing countries.

7.3. *The model of MBA education in China: Combination of economics and management*

Professor Lin Yifu also regards that a leader in the age of reform should perfectly handle both economics and management, only by which the leader can give full play to the "good timing, favorable geographical position, and good human relations" and create a new situation by innovation under the rapid reform. From the perspective of MBA education, economics studies include laws in society and economy, whereas management studies include internal management of the enterprise and marketing of products. BiMBA, organized by the Center, emphasizes on the combination of economics and management.

According to Professor Lin Yifu, economics should research the local problems of China. The Center proposes the explanation on the economic phenomena of China, instead of directly copying the theories of western economics. The Center not only combines economics and management but also puts forward its own theories to guide domestic MBA education courses. It is also helpful for economics students when teachers of the Center give lessons on management. The "People" is a vague image in traditional economics. Behind the economic phenomena of China stand individuals from various enterprises. Under the unstable situation, how would they think, how would they act, and what difficulties would they face? The economic theories should be abstracted from this level. Then the individual experiences can be applied to the large environment. The Center would propose the theories that can explain the changes in China, guide the students to view the macro environment and pattern with these theories, interpret their difficulties and successes and their positions in the environment, and enable them to estimate whether they can further succeed and what are the opportunities that they have. Only the theories that are proposed upon local phenomena are helpful for senior executives to become leaders, and, in addition, these theories also contribute greatly to the development of economics in China.

BiMBA is operated as part of the Sino-U.S. collaboration. The American side is experienced in standard management and utilization of the market environment, but it cannot seize the macro variation and they do not study philosophy. Compared to American partner's strength in teaching management, the Center is good at teaching economics. Some professors teach students with abstract ideas related to principles and make presentations on *Laozi* and *The Diamond Sutra* to teach students how to view phenomena with theories. According to the feedback from graduates, quite a few students find the "overall direction" in these courses very applicable. They regard them as a way of thinking, instead of ideology, which would facilitate them to make big policy judgment.

It is necessary and reasonable for BiMBA to win high appraisal in the market despite its small scale in China and other developing countries.

In the 2005 Dean Panel Session of the Institutes of Commerce and China, a journalist proposed a question for the deans of institutes of commerce: "I had an interview with a town entrepreneur several days ago, who just obtained his MBA degree. I asked what he learned, and he answered 'no' with a painful expression. I mentioned the expression, because some may answer 'no' in a frank expression. For example, the town entrepreneur is a typical representative in the process of rural urbanization, and what things can you give him?" Deans gave different answers, such as, "The institutes of commerce are gas stations"; "Management has no sufficient condition"; "Changing market demands necessarily lead to different management ideas"; "MBA is the improvement in knowledge and experiences"; "Problems lie in the examination system"; and so on. However, no one answered the question with "The town entrepreneur is a typical representative in the process of rural urbanization, and what things can you give him?"

Localization of MBA education in China is not a brand new concept. Many institutes of commerce are localizing the education, but are only limited to the establishment of the case library and recultivation of teachers. By comparison, BiMBA is more profound in the localization of MBA education.

It is extremely urgent to carry out the localization and reconstruction of the MBA education in China.

8. Lessons from the West and the Challenges and Opportunities of Chinese Economics[6]

I am delighted to have returned to the Renmin University of China to discuss the problems in imparting education in economics. I remember

---

[6]This chapter was originally the speech made on the seminar of "Modern Education on Economics: Inheritance of Commonness and Highlight of Individuality" held at the Renmin

that I once wrote an article entitled *Localization, Normalization, and Internationalization* for the 40th anniversary of the *Economic Research* in 1995, when I proposed that Chinese economists should conduct research on China's local problems with a standard approach, so that the research results could contribute to the development of international economics. Meanwhile, I estimated that the 21st century would witness most of the experts in economics emerging from China.

It has been 10 years since I proposed the estimation. Upon reviewing the proposal at that time, I feel more confident about the estimation. I considered that the 21st century was to be the century of the Chinese economists, because any theories of economics are the simple logic system utilized to explain and explicate the economic phenomena. The logic of most important theories is generally simple, so the importance of these theories cannot be determined by the logic itself, but is decided by the importance of the phenomenon explained by the theory. The more important the phenomenon, equally more important is the simple logic system that can explain the phenomenon.

The status of the Chinese economy and Chinese economic phenomena has become increasingly important in the global economy. Although China's economic size amounts to only one-eighth that of America, based on the exchange rate, the annual economic growth is three or four times that of America. Based on the purchasing power parity, China's economic size has exceeded America by half. In terms of international trade, China has become the second largest trading country, with an annual growth rate of 25% in foreign trade after its entry into the World Trade Organization (WTO). The economic and trade growth of China have affected many countries of the world, leading to the wave of China craze in the recent one to two years. China's story of rapid economic growth was published in all major media and magazines at great length. Many globally influential economists, including the Nobel Prize winner Joseph E. Stiglitz, started visiting China often. The reason for the China craze is the increasing influence of China's economic development on the world economy, and everyone wants to understand China's economic phenomena.

University of China on March 18, 2006. It was originally published in the *Newsletter of the China Center for Economic Research of Beijing University*, 16th issue, 2006 (578th issue of history).

Another factor contributing to my estimation that there would be more masters of economics coming from China lies in that the Chinese economic phenomena provides many opportunities for theoretical innovations. In addition to the large economic size and important economic phenomena, economists have to innovate the theories before they become experts. Theoretical innovations are always derived from phenomena that cannot be explained with the existing theories. Take the theory of the macroeconomics as an example. The Great Depression, which occurred in the developed countries in the 1930s, could not be explained with the theoretical frame of the neoclassical balance between the supply and demand — this gave birth to the Keynes macroeconomic theory. The stagflation occurred in the 1960s when inflation did not increase the employment rate or improve the economic growth rate as estimated by Keynes — the rational expectancy theory emerged. By the 1990s, economists found that the government could conduct fine adjustment on economy with monetary and financial policies, so the neoclassical synthesis theory and the new Keynes theory emerged.

Since the reform and opening up, there were many phenomena that cannot be explained by the existing theories. Two examples are given here. Firstly, China adopted the evolutionary reform featured with the "double-track system" and obtained a 10-year constant rapid economic growth by the late 1980s, but in fact, the mainstream economics circle generally held a pessimistic view on the double-track system reform and considered that big problems might emerge at any time. It was commonly accepted by the mainstream economics circle that the socialist planned economy was not as good as the capitalist market economy, the double-track system economy was not as good as the original planned economy, and the "shock therapy" based on the "Washington Consensus" should be applied in the reform of the socialist planned economy. This is because institutional guarantee was necessary for the effective operation of an economic system, including the market-decided prices, private property rights, and balance of budget by the government. Economists show different opinions on many problems, but as recorded in an article by Larry Summers, the mainstream economists surprisingly reached a consensus on how to conduct reform in the planned economy. However, China's annual economic rate had reached 9% from 1978 to 1990, while it had increased to 9.9% between 1990 and 2005. The collapse or stagnation as estimated by many mainstream economists did not appear. The Soviet Union and Eastern Europe adopted the "shock therapy", but it led to economic collapse and stagnation, instead of rapid economic growth as estimated by the mainstream economists. Even after 10 years, many countries were not restored to the level before the transformation; and Eastern European countries of better performance were nothing far from the performance of China.

One recent instance is that between 2000 and 2002, many economists considered that China's economic growth rate figures were false, because deflation broke out in China in 1998, leading to constant decline of the commodity prices. Deflation in foreign countries would generally lead to a sluggish economy, with nil or even a negative growth rate, only a little higher than zero as supported by the government's strong financial policies. The most typical instances are the Great Depression in America in the 1930s and the deflation in Japan in 1999. However, China's economic growth rate had reached 7.8% in 1998, 7.1% in 1999, 8.0% in 2000, 7.5% in 2001, and 8.0% in 2002, making China the country of the most rapid economic development. However, some foreign economists did not believe in the validity of China's GDP growth rate. In addition, China's energy consumption had dropped by 0.8% in 1997, 4.1% in 1998, and 1.6% in 1999. It was commonly believed that under such a rapid growth, with a rate of 7% or 8%, the energy consumption should also increase, compared to China's decrease in energy consumption. Therefore, they doubted China's economic growth rate. Professor Thomas Rawski at the University of Pittsburgh wrote an article stating that China's economic growth rate should be 3% at the maximum, probably near zero, which had been widely referred to in domestic and foreign academic circles. As several years have passed, domestic and foreign economists now commonly accept that China's economic growth rate should be higher, instead of lower, than the published figure.

As seen from the above instances, the estimations of many foreign mainstream economists on the Chinese economy have been proven to be untrue. For the argument on the validity of China's economic growth rate proposed by Thomas Rawski, some people stated that he was only an observer, but not a top economist. However, most mainstream economists, including many experts in economics, recommended "shock therapy" to the Soviet Union and Eastern European countries and believed that such a therapy would help them in the rapid transformation and improvement of efficiency and wealth in the short term. They also held a pessimistic view on China's double-track system reform. These experts prescribed for and estimated on important economic issues, which proved to not be in accordance with the facts. Only two possible reasons could be found: (i) they did not understand economics and (ii) problems exist in many current theories of economics. These experts had developed many new theories in modern economics, so they definitely knew economics. Therefore, the problems should lie in many theories of modern economics.

Many theories in economics textbooks and mainstream literatures were unable to explain the transformation of China and the Soviet Union and Eastern Europe, and they were also not able to explain many problems that China faced during its economic development. After WWII, most developing countries had obtained political independence and started to pursue economic development independently. However, as known to all, the countries that formulated the policies for economic development based on the mainstream development economics at that time have suffered poor economic development, while the economic policies applied by Asia's "Four Little Dragons" and Japan, who performed well in economic development, were negated by the mainstream theories of development economics at that time.

Compared to the 1950s and 1960s, modern economics has made many theoretical progresses both in economic growth and development. However, do these theories really reveal the reasons for the success or failure of the economic development? For example, the neoclassical growth theory emphasized on the accumulation of materials and capitals, but the endogenous economic growth theory turned to focus on the role of the accumulation of human capital on technological innovation as well as the scale economy and believed that they were the key to the success and failure of a country's economic growth. However, Asia's "Four Little Dragons" and Japan, which had succeeded in catching up with strong countries, were lower in their education level and smaller in their economic size than the developed countries. Human capital definitely plays a very important role in the economic growth, but it cannot be regarded as the key decisive factor. This is because the East Asian economies, which have lower levels of human capital and are smaller in size, had caught up with or narrowed the gap to developed countries. In addition, the education level among the socialist countries in Soviet Union, Eastern Europe, and Cuba could be compared to or even surpassed developing countries such as

Europe and America, but their performance in economic development was not strong. If the planned economic system was blamed for the situation in socialist countries, the Philippines could be used as another instance. The Philippines adopted capitalist market economy and democratic system and enjoyed a high level of education, but its performance in economic development was very poor. Therefore, the endogenous economic growth theory may also fail in unveiling the most important decisive factor for the success or failure of the economic development of developing countries.

After the heat of endogenous economic growth theory, the new hot spot is on the decisive role of the system on economic development. The research focus lies in how the systems of different American colonies that were formulated upon special environmental conditions 300 or 400 years ago affect the current economic development of the American countries. The theory on whether the institutional conditions that prevailed 300 or 400 years ago could decide the current economic development has little effect on changing the fate of a developing country, because these institutional conditions cannot be changed now. In addition, American countries are still changing. For example, Chile's economic development was as poor as other Latin American countries in the 1970s, but has seen sound economic development after the reform in the 1970s. The institutional conditions that prevailed 300 or 400 years ago are unchangeable and the unchangeable condition cannot be utilized to explain the changing situation. Therefore, the current hot spot of development economics has also not touched the key factor that decides the economic development of a developing country.

Modern economics also suffers the same difficulty in the problems of reform and development. William Easterly, the former chief economist of the World Bank, published an article entitled *The Lost Decades* in 2001, which discussed on the achievements made by most developing countries that conducted reform based on the "Washington Consensus" as guided by the International Monetary Fund (IMF) since the early 1980s. According to him, in terms of the main variable that decides the performance of a country's development in modern economics, these developing countries have made huge improvements, such as the balanced government budget, open market, and free finance, but they have not seen changes in economic growth and the status of macroeconomy. He found out that the median per-capita GDP growth rate of these developing countries was 2.5% in the

1960s and 1970s, but decreased to zero in the 1980s and 1990s, while the fluctuation of macroeconomy was even more serious in the 1980s and 1990s compared to the 1960s and 1970s.

Regarding the reform and development problem that is closely related to China, many theories of modern economics on reform and development cannot explain the successes and failures in China's economic reform and development and can hardly explain the successes and failures of other developing and transforming countries. However, I believe that any economic phenomenon that cannot be explained by the existing theories does not necessarily mean that the phenomenon cannot be explained by theories at all. When a phenomenon cannot be explained by the existing theories, then it is actually the best chance for theoretical innovation. A theory itself is, in fact, a simple logic system. Only a few social and economic variables can be maintained in the logic system, so it is important to confirm which variables should be kept in the theory. I think that, owing to the geographical factor, Chinese economists have a better understanding on the problems of China and other developing and transforming countries than economists of developed countries. Actually, this is a rarely seen opportunity for Chinese economists to conduct innovations on theories of economics and contribute to the development of economics.

However, Chinese economists have to overcome many challenges in order to turn their opportunities into reality. Modern economics is considered the most popular subject by Chinese students who want to govern and benefit the people by studying it. After the Opium War in 1840, China had suddenly changed from a celestial empire to a poor and backward country. As stated by Professor Huang Renyu, intellectuals in modern history have had two goals: (i) saving the nation and (ii) strengthening the country. When the nation was invaded by foreign powers, they tried to save the nation but when the nation finally came to peace, they spared no effort to make the nation prosper. Adam Smith published the *Wealth of Nations* in 1776, which was the start of the modern economics. Adam Smith discussed on how to make a country rich. Therefore, Chinese students wholeheartedly want to learn modern economics by learning lessons from the west and hope to learn the true principle to help China become stronger.

The problem is that the lessons from the west may not be applicable to China. Any theory of economics or other social sciences is not the truth, because the causality discussed in the theoretical model only comes into existence under certain restrictive conditions, but cannot be applied universally. As a developing and transforming country, China shows a great gap to developed countries in culture, social systems, legal frameworks, material conditions, and market growth level. The experiences that are applicable in developed countries may not be applicable in China owing to the differences in conditions. Moreover, theories of modern economics themselves are constantly developing. The economic growth theory comes from the neoclassical growth theory, new growth theory, and the new institutional system, while the macroeconomic theory has developed from Keynesianism, rational expectancy theory to neoclassical synthesis theory. Theories make progresses by negating the previous theories. What lessons should we learn from the west to apply in China? We, as the teachers, have to be clearly aware that it is a very difficult and challenging job to truly contribute to China's reform, development, and modernization.

Teachers should first change their education methodologies and way of thinking in order to overcome the above-mentioned challenges in performing research. Currently, as affected by the thinking model of "learning lessons from the west", many excellent university teachers generally copy the foreign theories, summarize them, sort them out, and explain them. When I returned to China in 1987, I was constantly asked to introduce the most advanced theories of foreign countries. Their hunger for knowledge was appreciated, but the teaching method that pursues the frontier economics is inappropriate, as the education on economics aims to help students understand the economic phenomenon in China, estimate the evolution of the phenomenon, and avoid or change the phenomenon based on the understanding and estimation. The frontier theories of modern economics are generally proposed by economists in developed countries, often to explain the phenomenon in the developed countries. The phenomena may vary in characteristics, so the theories may not be applied in China. Although some frontier theories may be proposed for problems in developing and transforming countries, they may not come to the desired end, since economists in developed countries have no own experiences on the social, economic, cultural, and political factors of the developing and transforming countries. If the education is conducted based on the traditional thinking model of "learning lessons from the west", the education on economics may become ideological and dogmatic, as said by Professor Stiglitz, which may mislead the students.

The 11th Five-Year Plan just approved emphasis on the independent innovation, which is also needed in economics and other social sciences. For the better teaching of economics, teachers have to conduct in-depth research on the situation of China's economic reform and development, understand the phenomena, and summarize and abstract the theory that can explain the practical problems in China. Only teaching in this way, not being ideological or dogmatic, can help students understand China's economic phenomena and problems.

The education on economics should be aware that any phenomenon can be observed in many aspects, so many different theories are proposed to explain one phenomenon. Some of these theories may be competing, i.e., if one is correct, the other one should be wrong; while some of them are relatively complemented, i.e., they are both correct and complementing each other. Even though a teacher proposes a correct theory that can be used today, it will be of no use in the future because China's society and economy are constantly developing. Laozi, a famous philosopher of Taoism, once said that "the way that can be told of is not an unvarying way". Therefore, the teachers should teach the students the method to view and analyze problems, instead of the existing theories that can be applied right after their graduation. The unique and unchanged in economics is that "a policy maker will make his best choice within his selection scope", which is the fundamental assumption for "rationality". Various theories can be generated to explain various phenomena from the special perspective of economics.

The most important is to help students build a rational viewpoint to observe problems in order to teach them the method to view and analyze problems. However, the education on economics also needs to refer to the theories put forward by domestic and foreign economists. Only with these theories can the teacher help students understand the scope of economics, but teachers should highlight that these theories are only the application cases for the rational viewpoint to analyze problems. Owing to similar restrictive conditions and similar specific problems with China, some theories can be referred to, while some others should not be directly imitated.

The education on economics for the undergraduates mainly aims to teach students not to explain the economic phenomenon with existing theories, but to observe the phenomenon from a rational viewpoint. The education on economics for graduate students should, in addition, train their ability to abstract the phenomenon they are observing and present the causality with rigorous logic, better to build a logic model with mathematics commonly accepted by the mainstream economics circles. Secondly, as long as a phenomenon can be explained by a theory of internal logic self-consistency, the phenomenon can be combined with different restrictive conditions and explained by more theories of internal logic self-consistency. Many of these theories compete with each other. Therefore, graduate students should be trained to collect and sort out statistics and examine the deductions of the theoretical models based on metering method in order to verify their own theories and others theories. Only through this can an innovation-oriented education on economics be built.

9. The Methodology of the Pursuit of Knowledge[7]

The following are excerpts from the author's speech made in the Yuanpei Class in 2002:

Mr. Zhu Qingsheng and students, it is a pleasure for me to exchange with you from the Yuanpei Class my experiences on the pursuit of knowledge. The Yuanpei Class is an important experiment from Beijing University in this new century. As the highest seat of learning, Beijing University should lead the new age and start a new trend, including the education reform.

The traditional model of the Soviet Union significantly affected China's education in the planned economy stage. Students of senior high school should choose from science and arts. The university entrance examination is subdivided into disciplines and majors. This kind of education was necessary in the special planned economy age. When New China was founded in 1949, China was still a very backward agricultural economy. Only a few people were educated, but experts were needed in various industries to rapidly build China as a modern industrial economy. Therefore, the goal of undergraduate education at that time was to quickly cultivate a batch of students who could immediately play their roles once they started their work. The enrollment at universities was confirmed by the demands of construction projects and industries in the future. Students had to learn some knowledge and skills that could be immediately applied once they

---

[7]This chapter was sorted out according to the record of the speech made in the Yuanpei Class on November 10, 2002. It was originally published in *Newsletter of the China Center for Economic Research of Beijing University*, 12th issue, 2003, (354th issue of history).

started work. After graduation, these students would be allocated according to the plan. A student's role would not change significantly during his or her life.

In the more than 20 years since the reform and opening up in 1978, China has transformed from its original planned economy system to the market economy system. Different than the period of planned economy system, China would face a society of rapid changes in industrial, employment, technological, and rural and urban structures, as well as globalization. Each person may participate in different kinds of jobs, from the secondary industry to the tertiary industry, or from the labor-intensive industry to capital-intensive industry. They should master new knowledge and techniques in the same industry. Therefore, the goal of the undergraduate education is to cultivate students' capacity of constant learning, instead of the professional skills of a certain work position. Beijing University sets up the Yuanpei Class to provide you with a wide and deep foundation to enable you to constantly absorb new knowledge and adapt to the changing work needs in the market economy of rapid variation. In the more than one year after its establishment, Yuanpei Class has gained great success and social recognition. Students of Yuanpei Class in 2002 have shown very good performance, and we hope that you can make an even better performance under the guidance of Mr. Duan, Mr. Zhu, and other teachers. We also hope that the experiences from the new experiment can be employed to promote educational reform at Beijing University and form a new model for the national higher education.

As a teacher at Beijing University, I feel honored to be the tutor of the Yuanpei Class and involved the experiment of Yuanpei Class. I was asked by Mr. Zhu to meet with you and exchange some opinions, and since then, I have thought about what I should discuss. Han Yu once stated in *On the Teacher* that "a teacher transmits the methodology, imparts knowledge, and resolves doubts". "Imparting knowledge" refers to teaching professional knowledge, such as economics, laws, sociology, physics, and chemistry, etc. "Resolving doubts" means to answer students' questions. There are teachers, respectively, responsible for the courses of each department, who will impart knowledge and answer questions on professional knowledge, and the tutor of Yuanpei Class shares no main responsibility on this. Therefore, I want to talk about the "methodology" mentioned in *On the Teacher*.

What is the "methodology"? The methodology here refers to the goal, principle, and method to handle oneself, handle affairs, and pursue the knowledge. To handle oneself, handle affairs, and pursue knowledge show different emphases, but according to my own experiences, the three share many similarities. As the tutor of Yuanpei Class, I will start with the pursuit of the knowledge.

How does one pursue the knowledge? Confucius indicated in the *Analects of Confucius* that "learning without thought is useless; and thought without learning is dangerous". According to Confucius, a man is not confused till the age of 40, but from the age of 50, a man knows the fate decreed by heaven. I am in my 50th year now, and having studied in the Beijing University, taught students, and conducted research for many years, I am still not able to understand the meaning of the two: "learning" and "thought". *The Doctrine of the Mean* advocated "extensive learning; thorough inquiry; careful reflection; clear discrimination", which is the best explanation for these words.

"Learning without thought is useless". Here, the "learning" refers to the learning of the existing theories. "Extensive learning" is required. As the theory is formed to explain the phenomenon, observations in different points of view on the same phenomenon may lead to different theories, which share commonness, meanwhile showing different focuses. Therefore, we should not only follow the statements of only one school but should also conduct "extensive learning".

However, the "extensive learning" is not enough. Learning without thinking can only enable the person to become a "walking encyclopedia". Moreover, among current theories, some are true and some are false. Theories and doctrines often come into conflict. People may become more confused if they remember all these theories.

How to make the "extensive learning" useful? This depends on "thorough inquiry". Two principles should be followed in the "thorough inquiry". Firstly, any theory is utilized to explain the phenomenon, so causality is required. Only a theory of internal logic self-consistency can tell us the cause, the mechanism, and the effect, while the effect is the phenomenon to be explained. When learning the theory, we should firstly examine the self-consistency of the internal logic, before we decide whether or not to accept an existing theory. Therefore, tutors of the Yuanpei Class have come to a consensus to focus on the training of logic for you.

Students learning natural science have a better foundation in mathematics, especially the rigorous logic of mathematics, so they have fewer problems in this aspect. Students learning social science should attach importance to the cultivation of good logic thinking. You should not only be attracted to new ideas but you should also reject the new ideas that are without internal logic self-consistency. Secondly, the theory is used to explain the phenomenon. Therefore, in addition to the requirement on the internal logic self-consistency, it is also required that the deduction based on the logic of the theory accords to the phenomenon to be explained. If it disagrees with the phenomenon, the theory is proved to be false and should be abandoned. A phenomenon can be explained by many theories and deductions at the same time, since many theories may infer to the same result as the phenomenon. Then we should further make certain theories that are complementary and competing. Complementary theories can be all correct at the same time, which means that the phenomenon may be created by different causes, so we have to figure out which cause is the most important or which cause is playing the most important role. Competing theories cannot all be true at the same time, so the deductions of these theories should be examined to confirm which theory should be temporarily accepted and which theory should be abandoned. A theory can only be temporarily accepted when its deductions have not been proved to be false by the experiences.

People of extensive learning should follow Mencius's critical spirit of "better not read a book at all than trust it completely" and put efforts on "thorough inquiry". They should not only pay attention on the originality and internal logic self-consistency of a theory, but should also pay attention on the uniformity between the theoretical deductions and the phenomenon.

Students of Beijing University are strongly responsible for the social development of China. We should not only learn the existing theories and understand the previous phenomena leading to the theories but should also explain the new phenomena and promote the social reform and development. The *Analects of Confucius* proposed that a teacher should gain new knowledge by reviewing the old knowledge. Faced with the constantly changing society, students of Beijing University should also follow the principle to be capable of leading various industries. However, since the society is constantly changing, can we explain the new phenomena by learning the old theories that are summarized based on the previous phenomena? In ancient times, a person crossed the river by boat. If his sword fell into the water, he nicked at the side of the boat and hoped to find his sword where the snick was. Was he right to try and retrieve his sword? The answer depends on many objective conditions, such as whether the boat and water were moving or not. If the boat was docked and the water was not moving, or was moving slightly, the passenger could leave for a while and look for the sword according to the snick, and he could possibly find the sword. If the boat was in the water when the boat and water were moving, the sword could not be found. Essentially, any theory is a kind of "nicking on the boat". If the given conditions are not changed, the theory can explain and estimate the phenomenon, but no theory is the whole truth because the society is constantly changing similar to the flowing water. Laozi stated at the beginning of the *Classic of the Virtue of the Tao* that "the way that can be told of is not an unvarying way", which reminds us that no theory can be universally applied. The same principle was also illustrated in the *Diamond Sutra* of Buddhism.

Then, how is new knowledge to be gained? The key is the word of "thought" in the sentence "thought without learning is dangerous". The "thought" here refers to "careful reflection", not quite similar with the "thought" of "learning without thought is useless", which refers to the "thorough inquiry". The "thought" in the latter sentence means the thinking activity to directly observe the phenomenon and understand the behind logic of the phenomenon. Why should we be "careful" in this "thought"? It is because intellectuals often observe phenomena based on the existing theories. However, even if the new phenomenon emerging along with the development and change of the society agrees with the logic inference of the existing theories, it does not prove that the phenomenon is the effect led by the cause revealed by the existing theories. If we are not careful enough, we may possibly make mistakes. We should be careful in two aspects. Firstly, carefully observing the phenomenon, avoid carelessness, and seeing what comes from one small clue. Secondly, during the observation of the phenomenon, we must remind ourselves to not be restricted by the existing theories. We should not be enslaved by the existing theories, breaking the restrictions, and directly analyzing and understanding the stories behind the phenomenon. The explanations reached upon the "careful reflection" may be the same with the existing theoretical explanations, but the explanation was constructed based on our personal experiences, similar to the scholar who proposed the existing theory instead of the simple acceptance of knowledge, so we have a more profound understanding over the phenomenon and theory. In addition, by preventing the effect of existing theories, we may find a different logic for the phenomenon and gain new knowledge.

Any scholar who wants to propose creative ideas should cultivate his ability to directly see the causality behind an observation of the phenomenon. Each society is featured with many social and economic factors, but an important social and economic phenomenon is generated upon a few important factors. In addition, a theory is a tool of information conservation, so it should be as simple as possible. Fewer factors maintained in the theoretical model would be better. Many of the thousands of social and economic factors have no direct relation, or little relation, to the generation of the phenomenon to be explained and should be given up. Variables that are related to the phenomenon also have different roles — some as the exogenous causes, some as the endogenous causes created by exogenous causes acting as the intermediate variable for the phenomenon, and some as the effect accompanied with the emergence of the phenomenon that created the exogenous causes. A theory should be established upon the most fundamental exogenous cause, which can be of the greatest explanatory power, and the inferences can be tested by various experiences and phenomena. However, which is the most fundamental and exogenous cause among these large amounts of social and economic factors? Without the ability of "clear discrimination", we may be more confused as we observe the phenomenon and think about the causality behind the phenomenon regardless of all these existing theories. Therefore, "learning" is required. The "learning" in the "thought without learning is dangerous" shows different emphasis compared to the "learning" in the "learning without thought is useless". I think that the "learning" in the "thought without learning is dangerous" has two meanings. Firstly, "learn the method to observe the phenomenon and reveal the causality behind the phenomenon". The methodology of proposing theories based on the observation of phenomena is applicable for all subjects. According to the *Great Learning*, "Things have their root and their branches. Affairs have their end and their beginning. To know what is first and what is last will lead near to what is taught in the *Great Learning*". This is universal for all subjects. The unchanged factors can be ignored for the explanation of a phenomenon. For factors that have been changed, we should make it clear which factor changes first. The factors that change before the emergence of the phenomena may be the important clue and the breakthrough point for the problems, though they may not necessarily be the fundamental cause for the phenomenon. In addition, some methods vary in different subjects. For economics, the methodology often refers to the study of a rational person's choice made under certain restrictive conditions. Therefore, the fixed methodology for theories on economics can be summarized later. Firstly, make clear who the policy makers are, governmental officials, enterprise managers, staff, or consumers. Secondly, make clear what the policy makers' goal is, maximizing the efficiency, including incomes and wealth, minimizing the risks, improving the social status, or inner satisfaction. Thirdly, make clear which variables can be selected by the policy makers to realize the goal. Fourthly, make clear the opportunity of the selection. A theory on economics consists of the above-mentioned four elements, while an economic phenomenon often refers to the result of one or more kind of policy makers' choice of the different portfolios or changes of the latter three elements. A discerning economist observes problems based on the four elements. The second meaning of "learning" is to "learn the existing theories relevant to the phenomenon", which aims to find out the similarities and differences between our own theories and the existing theories instead of to explain the observed phenomenon with the existing theories. If our own theory is different within the existing theories, then the "careful reflection" should be conducted to examine the self-consistency of our own theory and confirm whether the theoretical inference accords to the known experiences and phenomena. If no problem exists in the two aspects, we should further analyze whether our theory is complementary or competing with the existing theory. After all these procedures, we can understand the new point of our explanation and its contribution to the theory contents. If the existing theoretical explanation is totally with our own, we can profoundly understand the phenomenon and causality without confusion, though we have not innovated on theories.

If you, the students of the Yuanpei Class, are diligent in "thinking" in your studies and lay a solid foundation in "learning", you will welcome many opportunities to make initiative contributions to the development of theories on your own subjects. New theories are derived from new phenomena. China is developing in a tremendous change that has never before been seen in history, which gives rise to many new phenomena in every subject. On one hand, China has transformed from the planned economy to the market economy, and on the other hand, China has transformed from a rapidly developing and agricultural economy to modern economy, both of which have been completed in a very short time. According to the study in 1991 by the World Bank in the *World Development Report* on the cases of successful economic development after the Industrial Revolution in 1991, it took Britain 58 years from 1780 to double the per-capita production, 47 years for America after 1839, 34 years for Japan after 1885, 18 years for Brazil after 1961, 11 years for South Korea after 1966, and 10 years for China after 1977. The growth rate of China's per-capita income had been even more rapid in the late 1980s and 1990s. We know that most theories by now are proposed by scholars from developed countries. The theory proposed by each scholar aims to explain the phenomena observed by the scholar, so the theories put forward by scholars of developed countries are utilized to explain the phenomena in developed countries. Owing to different development stages, different social and economic environments, and different restrictive conditions, the causes for the same phenomenon may be different. It is not necessarily wrong for scholars of developed countries to explain the phenomena in developing and transforming countries with their theories, but most of these theories do not touch the key points and attempt ineffective solutions. Local scholars would be the ones that complete the theoretical innovation, but not the scholars of distant places, which are decided by the characteristic of the theory itself. As mentioned earlier, only a few social and economic variables can be maintained in the theoretical model, but only scholars growing up and living in the society can better handle which factors should be maintained and which should be abandoned. A foreign scholar that did not grow up or live in China could hardly discover the logic behind the economic phenomenon. It is the same with students that grow up in China, studied abroad, and worked in foreign countries after they get their doctorate degrees, who cannot attain prominent achievements on any field related to foreign social and economic phenomena. Therefore, though many economists obtained their undergraduate degrees in China, studied abroad after that, and worked in foreign countries, they have only made prominent achievements on mathematical economics and econometrics that are non-related to social and economic phenomena.

In terms of the research on China's social and economic phenomena, in addition to the geographical advantages, Chinese scholars can also make more important contributions to economics. As a logic system of self-consistency, the theory's contribution cannot be defined by the logic itself, but is determined by the significance of the phenomenon explained by the theory. The more important the phenomenon, the more important will be the theory. In the 18th and 19th centuries, masters that lead the world trend of philosophy and social science mostly came from Europe, while most masters showed up in America after World War I (WWI). Since the economy is the foundation for the superstructure, the world economic center was located in Europe between the Industrial Revolution and the start of WWI, so the most important social and economic phenomena of the world were the social and economic phenomena in Europe. Therefore, the theories that explained the social and economic phenomena in Europe were the most important. Then, most masters of philosophy and social science showed up in Europe owing to their geographical position. After WWI, America rose as the world economic center, so most masters of philosophy and social science came from America. Along with the improving economic status of China in the 21st century, Chinese civilization has again become powerful. It is possible for China to become the world economic center and world center of learning in place of America, so many masters would be Chinese in the future. As the seat of learning of China, Beijing University is responsible for cultivating the world masters. Yuanpei Class is an institutional innovation to usher in the new age. As the tutor of the Yuanpei Class, I hope that you can cultivate yourself to be the world master.

What is the difference between masters and general scholars? A master must have his own set of theoretical systems, involving many aspects. Although various aspects are incorporated in the system, the system is not simply made up by non-related or conflicted opinions, but is a perfect whole with these opinions integrated by a fundamental and consistent principle. Confucius and Zigong, Confucius's student, made a question-and-answer in the *Analects of Confucius*, which also presented the same opinion. Confucius asked Zigong, "Do you think that I remember all the knowledge because I put great efforts in learning?" Zigong answered, "Yes. Is that so?" Confucius answered, "No. I only have a principle to integrate all knowledge". What is the principle that integrates Confucius's theoretical system? The answer can be found in another section of the *Analects of*

Confucius in the dialog with Zeng Seng, another student of his, which refers to "the doctrine of loyalty and consideration for others". Similarly, Laozi had stated the same idea in the *Classic of the Virtue of the Tao*. The real master's theoretical system can explain many phenomena, but the core concept of the system is very simple. With the simple core concept as the starting point, the master's theoretical system would explain the most fundamental cause of various phenomena and explain how the fundamental cause acts on other social and economic variables and lead to the phenomena. Although Confucius, Laozi, and Sakyamuni's thoughts involve all aspects, such as life, society, and politics, Confucius integrated his theoretical system with "the doctrine of loyalty and consideration for others", Laozi integrated his ideological system with "inaction", and Sakyamuni with "emptiness".

However, the social and economic phenomena are complicated and constantly changing. How can a scholar begin to understand the fundamental causes behind various phenomena and form a theoretical system integrated with a simple core concept? *The Doctrine of the Mean* has proposed the answer as "The truth is not far from man. When men try to pursue a course, which is far from the common indications of consciousness, this course cannot be considered the truth". Without mankind, the universe is only a silent natural existence. The existence and subjective initiative of man give rise to various social and economic phenomena, so "the truth is not far from man". A master should be passionately concerned with society, including issues related to families, countries, and the world, and explain the fundamental of various phenomena in the current age. A scholar that only cares about his own interests can never become a master, even if he read thousands of books. When concerned about people and society, a master should view the matter from an overall perspective. As Wang Yangming[8] mentioned in his poem, a man can only avoid being smitten by the surface properties of the world from an overall perspective. Therefore, a master should be featured with confidence and a sense of vocation, and, therefore, he or she can establish the view of history and overall point of view and then see through the essence of various matters. At the same time, Mencius proposed that a master should have a high moral courage, because when

---

[8]Wang Yangming is a famous ideologist, philosopher, and militarist of the Ming Dynasty. He was the greatest master of heart study.

the master proposes a new idea and theoretical system that conflicts with the pre-existed and widely accepted theories, he will not be understood or accepted; he may even be criticized. Then courage is required, so that the master could debate with the existing theories and gradually teach the multitudes. Therefore, the same principle is required for one's own behavior and pursuing knowledge. The moral force, as the precondition for masters, is not inherent, but should be cultivated by oneself from time to time.

I mainly discuss on the pursuit of knowledge from the perspective of humanity and social science. The theories of natural science can be applied to societies of any essence and development stages, while their contributions can be defined according to an objective criterion. On the contrary, the contributions of theories on social science are determined by the importance of the phenomena explained by the theories in world politics and economics. However, the estimation that China would become the world center of learning in the 21st century, and the principle for the pursuit of knowledge can also be applied to the natural science. Since the research on natural science need large investment, more and more capitals would be invested to support the research on natural science, compared to the world along with the increasingly powerful economy of China. In addition, the wisdom and talents of the people in China would promote China's innovations on the theories of natural science. Both "learning" and "thought" are also important for the research on natural science, except that researchers of natural science think about the natural phenomena, instead of social phenomena. The master of the natural science should also contribute to many fields with his or her theories. It is said that Albert Einstein should have been awarded with 8 or 10 Nobel Prizes, because his relativity theory has significantly contributed to many branches of physics. Moreover, in the 21st century, more masters of natural science would come from China.

The Yuanpei Class is named after Mr. Cai Yuanpei, so you should put great efforts to live up to his name. Mr. Cai's days shared many similarities with current times, the age of great changes, and the age of transformation from block to openness. However, we are having better days than Mr. Cai. During his time, China had been invaded, bullied by foreign powers, and forced to open the gate from the Opium War to the May Fourth Movement, which was a "life and death" moment. At that time, the academic circle mainly reflected and criticized the traditional culture and introduced advanced foreign culture, systems, and theories. The whole nation was striving to save the nation and make it stronger, when it was impossible for them to summarize Chinese experiences to create a new trend for the human culture. In the previous 20 years, China has also transformed from isolation to openness, but it was our own choice. In addition, since the reform and opening up, China has become the country of the most rapid economic growth of the world, and seen the rapid approach of the great rejuvenation of Chinese nations. Economy is the foundation for the superstructure, and culture is the combination of economic foundation and superstructure. Along with the economic development, our social organizations, value systems, and lifestyles would change, and our culture would become the strong culture that is imitated and learned by other weak cultures. Most countries of the world are developing countries, which share the same thought to realize modernization and improve the living standards of the people. Therefore, the experiences of China's rapid economic development can be referred to by other developing countries. In the world history, China may become the first nation that develops from prosperity to decline and then again from decline to prosperity in the 21st century. It is a brand new cultural phenomenon that makes many theories on humanity and social science — which believed the human civilization would experience birth, old age, sickness, and death — inapplicable. This experience is also important for those nations at the cultural peak that may come to decline. We should take advantage of our geographical position to profoundly make the brand new cultural phenomenon clear. Compared to the scholars at Mr. Cai's days, it is the opportunity as well as the responsibility for Chinese scholars in the 21st century to make China a culturally developed country.

As the tutor for Yuanpei Class, I have high expectations for you. I think that the goal of the Yuanpei Class is to cultivate students of a higher level than the Oxford and Harvard Universities. Great Britain had passed its Golden Age and America is now a stable society. Chinese scholars embrace more opportunities than American and British scholars to make initiative theoretical contributions in the 21st century. In addition, Beijing University is stricter in selecting students than Oxford University and Harvard University. As many as more than 20 universities such as Harvard University exist in America, while the American population only amounts to one-fifth of China. In terms of the proportion, if Chinese students are as wise as American students, the students of Beijing University are more than 10 times qualified to become masters than the students of Harvard University. Confucius once indicated in the *Analects of Confucius* that teachers should teach students according to their ability and set higher goals for talented students. Students of Beijing University are all more talented and so the teachers of Beijing University should set a higher goal for these students than cultivating them in a similar level as in Harvard and Oxford Universities. Yuanpei Class is an experiment of Beijing University in the new century. Let us make joint efforts to make a fine job of Yuanpei Class and Beijing University, to usher in the age of Chinese masters on all subjects in the 21st century. Only by this, can we live up to our age and the name of Yuanpei Class.

Index

Printed in the United States
By Bookmasters